AN AMERICAN CHRISTMAS CAROL

A STORY OF CONVERSION AND REDEMPTION

K. RAPHAEL KINNEY

An American Christmas Carol
ISBN-13: 978-1-906628-10-9
Published by CheckPoint Press, Ireland

CheckPoint Press
Dooagh, Achill Island, Westport, Co Mayo
Republic of Ireland

Tel: +353 9843779 / Email: editor@checkpointpress.com

www.checkpointpress.com

FOR
MARY ANN

CONTENTS

PREFACE

Miracles are a retelling in small letters

of the very same story which is written

across the whole world in letters too

large for some of us to see.

C. S. LEWIS

PART THE FIRST

CHAPTER ONE

"Marley was dead, to begin with. There is no doubt whatsoever about that. The register of his burial was signed by the clergyman, the clerk, the undertaker and the chief mourner. Scrooge signed it and Scrooge's name was good upon change for anything he chose to put his hand to. Old Marley was as dead as a door nail."

The young lawyer closed the presentation copy of Charles Dickens' *A Christmas Carol* and placed it carefully on a corner of his massive desk. What a strange Christmas gift for a secretary to give to her boss, he thought. He made a mental note that there were only four days until Christmas, and he had yet to buy her a present, or any of the rest of the staff, for that matter.

His chief legal assistant, Joe Poleski, entered his office promptly at five p.m. to remind him of tomorrow's most urgent matters. Already the cold Chicago streets were pitch dark. He slipped on his expensive overcoat and stepped onto the elevator to descend the ten floors down to Wacker Drive. It was a long walk to his L station on Wabash, but he needed the exercise.

As he exited the lobby of his office building into the cold dark Chicago night, he silently cursed himself for forgetting his rubberized overshoes. "If I keep doing this, I'll ruin these shoes, and God knows how much they cost!" He mumbled to himself as he checked his reflection in the plate glass window. He noted with special satisfaction his extremely expensive, diamond-encrusted, Swiss-made gold watch. It had been a present from his law firm when he had made partner last year. Out of all of the accoutrements of his wealth, power and prestige, this watch said it all. No one could say that Michael Barron, Esquire did not know how to dress for success.

There was a bounce in his step as he began his trek across the Loop of Chicago, but it wasn't due to the cold. He had just learned the size of his annual year-end bonus check from a friend in the accounting department. It had exceeded even his grandiose expectations. No wonder, he thought to himself, he had been made full partner in the law firm of Kinwood, Smith, Nelson and Barron.

Then again, he deserved it. Michael had worked hard all his life, gone to all the right schools, joined the right tennis and country clubs, even made sure he was on the letterhead of the best high-profile charities in

Chicago. Nothing in this world, he thought, is an accident, which is why, many years ago, he had become an agnostic. "God helps those who help themselves." He chuckled under his breath.

The streets of Chicago blazed with the lights of Christmas glowing from retail shops displaying their finest wares. Michael could have afforded any of the products he saw that night as he hastened across the loop, but he always hesitated before he bought anything, for the price of an article was more important than the article itself. He knew what a good buy was and no one was going to fool him.

When he arrived at the entrance to his L stop, he paused in front of the old wood structure that served as a newsstand under the tracks. The smell of roasting chestnuts in the brazier next to the stand was appealing. So, with his evening newspaper, he purchased a small bag of the treats. He had purchased his evening newspapers for many years from this vendor, a middle-aged black man dressed in multiple layers against the cold. Of course, Michael had never bothered to learn his name. To him, he was simply one of the millions of people in this world who didn't have the drive, the energy, the brains, the education to soar as high as Michael had done. Michael was never condescending towards this old man, because to do so meant he would have to acknowledge him, and such people were well below Mr. Barron's perspective.

"And a good evening to you, sir, and a Merry Christmas," announced Emmitt to his regular customer. Michael thought he was only working him for a tip, so he didn't bother to reply. He turned toward the stairs to the elevated tracks; he hopped aboard his subway car, and with a practiced eye, looked over the inhabitants. He was looking for a vacant seat where he could spread out and thus discourage any of the unwashed masses from sitting next to him. It's too bad taxicabs are so expensive, he thought. Otherwise, I would never take this filthy mass transit.

It was only a short ride on the L before Michael arrived at his stop. He lived in a high-rise luxury condominium, very near the lakeshore on the north side. As he regained street level, he stepped off briskly up the street to walk the four or five blocks to his cross street. He passed a completely dark alley and did not notice a man stepping out behind him. The man moved slowly and simply stared at the back of Michael as he continued on his journey. He was short in stature with white, medium length hair and dark glasses. The stranger was dressed in a gray windbreaker with a white shirt, dark blue pants and black shoes; his clothing was totally inappropriate for the weather. The most amazing thing about this man was his skin. If Michael had turned around, he would've thought he was staring at an albino.

But he didn't turn around. In fact, he hastened his steps along that dark street on the north side of the city. This part of his evening commute was a little too dangerous for his tastes. The streets were poorly lighted, and he had heard of muggings in this area. His only concern was to get home as quickly as possible.

As he passed yet another alley, through his peripheral vision, he thought he saw some movement on the ground about 10 feet into the passage. He started to hesitate, thinking he should go back and investigate.

But his judicious nature got the better of him and he quickened his step. Before he could get more than a few feet further, however, he was stopped dead in his tracks by a strange noise.

It was a female's voice… a low moan… like a wounded animal.

CHAPTER TWO

At first he thought it was a mound of rags on top of the snow. But then he heard the moan again. It was definitely a woman and she was either drunk or hurt. Against his better judgment, he decided to investigate.

"Are you all right?" He asked immediately feeling stupid. Of course she wasn't all right!

As he inched forward, he noticed the condition of her old overcoat, topped with silver white hair. Even in the dim light of the alley, he could see the angry dark stain growing on her head. Blood, he thought.

He stepped out into the alley and quickly scanned the street for possible sources of help. A corner telephone booth, a passing police car would've sufficed, but there was nothing except the cold darkness of the December Chicago night around him. He heard the old woman's stir and meekly call for help. He turned and noticed that she had managed to sit up in a snow bank, bewildered and frightened.

"Don't worry. I'll get help!" He half—yelled at her. But she responded, "No, No. I'll be all right. Just help me to my feet."

"You need help, and you need it now." He said, assisting her, but she refused to listen to him and started to stumble out of the alley and down the street towards her home.

She didn't get too far. A few steps down the street, and she careened into the side of the building, barely maintaining her footing. Michael ran forward and grabbed her before she could collapse.

"I must call an ambulance," he said.

But she replied, "If I can just make it to my home. I'll be okay."

"Where do you live?" The young attorney inquired.

"Not far from here. A few blocks north, and then a few more blocks west. I can make it."

"Well, I'll walk with you at least part of the way to make sure." He replied. The few blocks she had described turned into a ten-block walk. But she seemed to gain strength as they walked along arm in arm.

They ended their walk in an old neighborhood of brownstone apartments. The old lady lived in a basement apartment at the front of the building. Michael helped her down the crumbling concrete steps through the basement door and into the front door of her tiny apartment. When she put her key into the door her legs finally gave out from the strain of the walk. As she began to collapse, Michael pushed open the door and carried her inside. He fumbled for the light switch, and when he flipped it he was amazed by what he saw.

It was basically a one-room apartment with a small bathroom and kitchenette. The only outside illumination came from two small windows, near the ceiling, that looked out upon the sidewalk in front of the building. The entire area smelled with the musk of an old basement. Of course, none of this surprised Michael. He had seen such circumstances, many times before. But he wasn't prepared for the books.

They were everywhere, from the floor to the ceiling, on every wall, on top of the bed and table and in neat piles around the bed. There were books, hundreds of books.

As he helped the old woman get settled into the large double bed that dominated the room, he couldn't help noticing some of the titles of the books that surrounded him. *Meditations* by René Descartes; *War and Peace* by Tolstoy; *Crime and Punishment* by Dostoevsky; *The True Believer*, by Eric Hoffer. "Not exactly light reading," he thought.

"My name is Sarah." She volunteered weakly. "And I am Michael… Michael Barron" he offered. Without asking for permission He entered the small bathroom in search of first aid supplies. He came back to her bedside and pulled up an old rocker. . " It doesn't look too bad Sarah," he observed, as he examined the wound on her head and began applying first aid.

"You're right, they only hit me once, to stun me and grab my purse." She explained.

"In any event, you're very lucky," he responded. "I really wish you'd let me call an ambulance."

"No, no. I really will be all right."

"Well," he said somewhat embarrassed. "Is there anything else I can do for you before I leave?"

"Perhaps you would be kind enough to put the kettle on? There are some biscuits on the top shelf over the stove as well. Will you join me?"

Perhaps it was the season, perhaps it was his loneliness, but Michael was in no hurry to leave. He did as she suggested and prepared a simple meal from what was available in her tiny kitchen. He sat down in the rocking chair next to her bed to share their refreshments. After Sarah had eaten, she became noticeably stronger and more focused.

She sat upright in her bad and focused directly on the young man. "And exactly who is my savior?"

"Me?" He asked, somewhat flustered. "I'm just an attorney. I was walking home to my condo by the lake when I heard your cries for help in the alley." He felt he was under the gaze of a seasoned police officer as she carefully took his measure by the cut of his clothes, his watch, and his haircut.

"Hardly a simple attorney, I would venture," said Sarah.

"And what about you?" Michael asked, wishing to change the subject as quickly as he could. She saw through his device, but allowed it to succeed.

"I'm just an old woman with no family, who works as an Aide at the hospital. As you can see, my only friends are long since dead." She swept her hand around the room to indicate the hundreds of classical books.

"Since the end of the second world war, when I came to America, my life has been one of service to other people, combined with an effort to educate my poor female brain," she said, with more than a touch of sarcasm.

The look in her eyes startled Michael. He had rarely seen such intelligence in a person's eyes.

They searched for common ground in their conversation, but it quickly became apparent that Michael with all of his first-class education was no match for this old Jewish woman. Mercifully for him, she quickly became fatigued and started to drift off. He decided to take his leave, resolving to drop by tomorrow to see how she was faring.

"Sarah is there anything more I can do for you before I leave?"

"Could you help me take off his old woolen sweater, so I can sleep?" She asked. He did so. As she lay back down into the bed, he noticed that her left forearm appeared to have a tattoo on it. When she closed her eyes, he leaned forward to read the faded blue writing by the light of her bedside lamp. He froze as he read the inscription on her arm:

FELD---HURE A436528.

CHAPTER THREE

ichael had a terrible night. He had seen enough documentaries on television regarding World War II to have some understanding of what Sarah had gone through. His night was filled with scenes of concentration camps, gas chambers and brutality. When he awoke in the morning, he was more tired than when he had retired to bed

As he got his morning cup of coffee, he cursed himself. Why did I ever get involved with that old woman last night?, He thought. He moved to the windows of his twelfth floor condominium. As he stood in the living room, he gazed out over the great Lake, and then south over downtown. It was another cold gray, Chicago morning, with limited visibility. The weather should have made his mood worse, but after the night before, his spirits couldn't get any lower.

He got himself dressed and steeled himself for a long day at the office. There was much work to do before the Christmas break in order to prepare for the January company meeting in Florida. He would have to rely more on his assistant Joe Poleski than ever before.

Being the first one in the office, as usual, he switched on the lights and walked from one end of the richly appointed suite to the other. When he entered his private corner office he gazed out the glass windows and noticed no improvement in the dismal weather.

And as usual, Joe was the second to arrive. He always called out a cheerful good morning as he entered the suite and went towards the kitchenette to make the morning coffee for everyone. Michael caught a glimpse of him walking down the hallway and noticed he walked with more of a limp than usual. Joe's long-standing diabetic neuropathy was clearly getting worse, as was his eyesight. Michael couldn't stand any imperfection in his business associates. He felt it reflected poorly on the image of the firm. He made a mental note. In the coming year he probably would have to get rid of Poleski.

The morning sped by with its usual frantic pace. He was planning on eating lunch at his desk as he often did, but today he felt the need for fresh air and to just stretch his legs. He'd decided he would quickly walk a few blocks from his office to a side street, which contained his favorite Chinese restaurant. Upon entering, the headwaiter ushered him to a small table along the wall. Immediately, there appeared an ancient Chinese waiter, who had waited on Michael many times before, and for some visceral reason, Michael could not stand.

The old man wearing his mask of permanent servility, greeted Michael in his heavily accented broken English. After wishing Michael the "happiest of afternoons." He inquired as to his order. Michael could barely hold in his contempt. He of course had no realization of what this old gentleman had gone through in his life. The persecution, the education he brought with him from China, the difficulty of making his way in such a foreign land. No. Michael didn't know any of this, and if he had, he would not have cared.

When the check came Michael actually considered not giving the old waiter a tip. But instead, out of the generosity of the season, he tipped him the minimum 10 percent. As he did so a movement in the window at the front of the restaurant caught his eye. He glanced up to see a white-haired man with sunglasses, dressed in a windbreaker peering around the edge of the window at him. Two things startled Michael: the paleness of the man's skin and the look of sorrowful disapproval on his face. Within a second or two, the white-haired man had disappeared around the edge of the building. But for some reason he could not explain, this insignificant event disturbed him greatly. He finished his lunch and quickly walked back to his office.

The afternoon flew by as quickly as the morning had done with the assistance of Joe Poleski and Michael's personal secretary, Helen McDougal. He was able to dispatch work that normally would have occupied two of his rather full days. When five o'clock rolled around, he loaded up his briefcase with work he wished to do at home and stepped briskly out into the cold night. This night, however, he decided to vary his routine and walk a few blocks over to West Washington St. to transverse the loop. He knew the route well, as he did all of Chicago, and halfway to his L stop, he knew he was coming across St. Peter's Franciscan church.

As he approached the church he could see the lights emanating from within, illuminating the sidewalk directly in front of the old edifice. The street itself of course, was pitch dark except for the occasional streetlight. But then he heard it. These damn Salvation Army bell ringers, he thought, they're on every block. He had already tossed a few coins into one of their red kettles that week, and after all, what more could they expect! Sure enough, as he approached the front of the church, He saw a figure clad in dark blue standing in front of the church ringing the bell into that windswept December night. He decided to move out as far as he could to the curb, to avoid having to face the Salvation Army. Michael did not see a pure white hand emerge from the darkness of the alley next to the church and make a quick movement. He slipped on the ice at the curb and went down to his knees. Immediately the person clad in blue was by his side offering a hand to lift him back to his feet.

"Are you all right, Sir?" She asked, and for the first time Barron realized it was a woman.

"Yes, yes. I am fine." Realizing now with disgust, he probably would have to fish out more coins for her kettle. But as he straightened himself up, he looked at her two hands supporting his arm. She wore cheap woolen mittens with their fingers partially exposed. When he brushed off his knees, he noticed her shoes, old navy blue shoes like a nurse would wear with the big toe virtually worn out of one of them. He couldn't help but be immediately aware of the contrast with his expensive clothing.

But then it happened. He straightened up and by the light coming through the front doors of the church, he saw her eyes. He literally froze. The face was framed with a Navy blue old scarf topped by a navy blue Salvation Army hat. She had long black hair, a look of compassion, sympathy and concern filled her face. But her eyes, her eyes... he had never seen a more beautiful woman in his life. And it wasn't just the fact that she was beautiful. It was something else, something else that he could not explain.... that pierced his very core.

Michael stammered out an apology for inconveniencing her. With an air of complete innocence she introduced herself as Maria. He offered that his name was Michael, but overcome with a certain amount of embarrassment, he forgot to tip her, and hurried on his way. Thirty feet away, he stopped and felt compelled to turn. She'd returned to her red kettle, but she stood facing him. When he turned, she smiled and waved her hand in a feminine way that burnt into his memory. He turned around without smiling back and hurried down the street into the dark of the night, totally oblivious to the importance of this chance occurrence.

❄ ❄ ❄ ❄ ❄

When Michael stepped off the L on the North Side of Chicago, he was determined to walk as quickly as possible to his condominium by the lake. His day had been long and unsettling and given the restless night he had endured, he welcomed going to bed early after a light supper. But when he approached the cross street that headed west towards Sarah's basement apartment, Michael was overcome with a feeling that it was his duty at least to look in after her. He decided to ignore the feeling, but, nevertheless, found his steps directed towards her apartment.

Upon reaching her apartment he bent over and attempted to peer through the basement window. He could see a light on inside, but nothing else through the thin curtains. He hesitated and then decided to quickly check in on the old lady. He descended the few steps, passed through the front door of the building, and found himself opposite the old wooden door leading to her tiny apartment.

For a moment, he paused, truly undecided whether he should proceed or not. Suddenly he noticed that the door was not only unlocked, but also slightly ajar. After a few more seconds of hesitation, he raised his arm to knock on the door. For the second time in as many hours, he did not understand the extent to which his life was about to change. But before he could knock he heard the old woman's voice.

"Come in Michael. I've been expecting you."

CHAPTER FOUR

ichael Barron slowly pushed the door open. It took his eyes a few moments to get used to the dark. Only one light bulb burned within. There sat Sarah in her bed. He was shocked by her appearance. She obviously had not done well in recovering from her ordeal the day before.

"I really must insist now Sarah, that I take you over to the hospital."

"Sit down Michael" she ordered, and he obeyed like a little child. She immediately adopted a more conciliatory tone and inquired. "And how was your day?"

"Well, he responded" kind of hectic, being the Christmas season and all." He wasn't sure at all where he stood with this old gentle lady. So he decided to go along with her.

"I am very happy you came today, Michael," she stated, sweetly. "It's sometimes very lonely for me here... What should we talk about this evening? Have you had your dinner?"

"Oh sure." He lied. "But can I get something for you? As always, he felt Sarah saw right through him.

"There are some cheese and crackers in the refrigerator and you could make some tea. That's all I really want."

He set to work at his task trying to decide how long he would stay for this short visit. As before, he sat in the rocking chair next to her bed while he served up their light snack. After a little nourishment she seemed to look better and certainly sound stronger.

"Yesterday we didn't have much chance to get to know each other. She responded simply. Perhaps you will be kind enough to tell me something about yourself while we dine on this sumptuous repast."

For the first time in a long time, Michael's guard was down. Normally, in talking with someone he was always trying to determine exactly what his or her alternative motives were, but he intuitively felt there was nothing to be on guard about with Sarah. And as is so often the case, a person will often tell a complete stranger things about their lives they wouldn't mention to their best friend.

"Well, there isn't much to tell you," he began, and then proceeded to ramble through his entire life: his early childhood on the North Shore of Chicago, his superior education, his career at the law firm, his awards and distinctions. All of which he was quite proud of, and he expected Sarah to be likewise impressed. She was listening intensely to his story, but not for the facts of his life. Rather if Michael had stopped for a moment he would have noticed her deeply intelligent eyes taking the measure of his heart and soul.

When he completed his long-winded exposition he paused to look with pride at Sarah expecting a barrage of questions and comments implying how well he had done. Instead, Sarah studied him for a moment and then quietly asked.

"Have you ever been married Michael? Do you have a family?"

The questions took him by surprise as if he considered them completely irrelevant. But after a moment he replied, he had very briefly, but they've gone their own ways. And as for his family, they all resided in a cemetery in Chicago. Sarah's eyes narrowed. She decided to change the subject. "Well, she said, my life certainly has been different than yours."

❋ ❋ ❋ ❋ ❋

Perhaps it was due to the fact that no one had shown any interest in this old immigrant's life in many a year. Or perhaps, once again it was just the loneliness of the season. But for whatever reason, Sarah decided to tell Michael her life story. She related how she'd grown up in Poland and was a young woman by the time the Nazis invaded her country. What had once been a simple red farmhouse isolated in a rural area of Poland became the infamous collection of concentration camps called Auschwitz. She and her family did their best to disguise their presence in Poland as Polish Jews. But the SS was very thorough, indeed. Eventually they were arrested. Most of her family stayed at Auschwitz proper. She and her twin sister were transferred to a nearby camp called Birkenau.

Because of the natural beauty of the two young girls they were turned into field prostitutes servicing the German troops. Eventually, however, they came to the attention of a certain SS doctor. He was a scientific researcher who specialized in the genetics of twins. What followed was unspeakable. Late one night the two sisters decided to escape. One sister made it, the other did not. Sarah lived in hiding on a Polish farm until the end of the war.

After the liberation she literally walked the entire way from the farm, upon which she was working as a laborer, to the German border. There, she slipped into occupied Germany, eventually making her way to England. Thanks to the aid from an underground society, she made it to America. The pseudo-scientific experimentation performed on her made her unable to ever have a family, which she admitted was probably a good thing, because after her experiences she was for many years emotionally crippled.

Michael gently interrupted her story. "After what you went through Sarah, I can't understand why you would decide to dedicate your life to helping others at the hospital or to engage in such a concentrated effort to educate yourself."

"On the contrary," she responded, "something happened when I was in the camps — something that led me on a lifelong pursuit of knowledge and understanding. Something that fired my enthusiasm in my weak attempt to help others.

Michael could see the ladies' mind working at lightning speed. Behind the chit chat and exchange of information between the two, something else was occupying her thoughts. It was as if she were trying to evaluate him. And make a decision.

There was a long period of silence, as Michael stole glances in order to watch Sarah's mind work. At times it was almost as if he were not in the room. Occasionally she would glance at him thoroughly. Her glance was so penetrating it made him uneasy. And then she would look away while processing the information.

Finally, she broke the silence and continued. "The first year I was in the camp, Michael, something happened that determine the rest of my life."

Michael's raised eyebrow, asked the question for him.

"Through the barbed wire that separated us girls from the men in the camp, I met a man… no, no it's not what you think! This man was much older than I but he was a prisoner, just like me. That was the only similarity. In fact, he was a Roman Catholic priest. Once a day we would contrive to meet near a certain spot with only the barbwire separating us. We would surreptitiously engage in conversation. This man became my confidant, my mentor, the one person who helped me cling to my sanity."

"What happened to him?" Michael asked.

"He was eventually executed by a firing squad of SS thugs. To the end, he never gave in to the Nazis. I actually had the misfortune of witnessing his execution. I can still see it as clearly as if it was yesterday. He stood with courage facing his own death, and with a look of forgiveness and pity on his face for his executioners.

"I saw many such crimes committed in Auschwitz, Michael, but this one was different. First this man had no reason to be executed. But secondly, he had taught me something that gave me hope and changed the very course of my life, regardless of all the suffering that was to come."

Once again Sarah lapsed into complete silence, and Michael had the common sense not to disturb her. She closed her eyes as if to take a brief nap. Michael debated slipping away, but he really had no place to go and for the first time in many, many years he actually felt that he was home.

❄ ❄ ❄ ❄ ❄

When Sarah awakened after her brief catnap she appeared focused and resolute. She asked Michael for some more tea, and as he got it she rearranged herself upright in the bed.

When Michael had taken his seat she turned slightly to face him and then said in a strong voice. "I have made my decision. Michael. I know we have only known each other for what," she glanced at the clock, "may be a total of six hours in the last two days. But I know my time is short. So you will be the one."

"What?" he blurted out. "The one? The one what?"

She smiled ever so slightly. "The one to receive the gift that I receive from that Catholic priest at Auschwitz so very, very long ago."

Michael stared at her and knew he was standing on the edge of a cliff. In a voice barely audible, he asked, "What gift?"

After an eternity, she responded:

"The Four Great Truths."

PART THE SECOND

CHAPTER FIVE

Happy the man who finds wisdom,
The man who gains understanding
For her profit is better than profit in silver,
And better than gold is her revenue.
Proverbs 3: 13, 14

Michael Barron stared at Sarah in disbelief. He had spent the better part of two evenings in this musty single room basement apartment during the busy Christmas season talking with what was obviously a mentally deranged woman.

He stared away at the wall behind Sarah's bed and broke into a derisive laugh. Well, the joke's on me, he thought. I'm just too kindhearted! I should have minded my own business. This woman is truly mentally unbalanced. The Four Great Truths, indeed.!

In a tone of voice he had not heard her use before, she said. "Don't be so arrogant, young man. Not all education and learning occurs in the great universities, despite what you might think!"

He snapped back to attention and stared at her hard. Seconds before, he was going to get up, make his excuses and leave never to see this old woman again. But there was something about this entire situation that he simply couldn't get his mind around.

He was the one to break the stare and the ensuing silence.

"Okay I'll bite," he said, with some derision, "What are the Four Great Truths?"

Sarah looked away again as if she was seeing well beyond the four walls of her little apartment, back, back through the years. Michael could see her mind was working at top speed. He understood she was trying to figure out what to say to him but he didn't understand that she was adjusting her thoughts to fit the comprehension of his mind.

Sarah decided that the Socratic method would be best with Michael, so she began with a question. Michael, what do you think is the one thing that all human beings have in common?

"Money, of course," he said flippantly.

Sarah's face flushed red. She was truly angry.

"I don't have time for such nonsense," she almost shouted at him. "Please be serious!"

The young lawyer was knocked off balance by the strength of her response. So he attempted to press what was obviously a losing argument.

"Well, you can't doubt that all human beings, every single one, are motivated by money." He said pompously.

Sarah softly replied, "Gandhi?"

"Okay, okay, I give up. What's the answer to your riddle?" Michael said half jokingly wishing to get on the woman's good side again.

Her face instantly flashed red again and her old blue eyes tore through him. "We are not playing a game!" She said. "What I am trying to impart to you will be to your advantage, not mine."

"Right, he responded to mollify the woman." He thought for a moment, his mind racing back to his early college days; the courses he had taken in the Humanities, Philosophy, and Psychology. He seemed to remember that all human beings have some sort of ' hierarchy of needs.' Eventually he tried a new approach.

"Well I guess there are many things human beings have in common," he finally said. "Everyone's looking for recognition, love, security, and yes, material gain."

Sarah stared at him in amazement as if to say, "This is all you have learned?"

She thought for a moment and then began a new more conciliatory approach.

"Of course you are correct," Sarah stated, " But if you look a little more closely at the question, you will understand that not all human beings are motivated by the same thing. Whereas, we all have one thing in common. There is one overriding fact of human existence on this planet. It's so obvious that most people forget it in their daily search for the things you mentioned."

"Can you think of it?"

Once again Michael ran through all the possible candidates. He actually thought. "It is a pretty good question, what do all human beings have in common?" The possible answers tumbled through his mind. Money, power, sex, love, family, security, food, shelter, pleasure and pain, greed and fear. He was now into the spirit of this little game and thought to himself. "It's just a riddle. I wonder what she thinks the answer is?"

Finally, he sat up in his rocking chair and looked at Sarah. "The answer to your riddle," he announced pompously, "is the pursuit of pleasure and the avoidance of pain." This line was so good, he actually saw himself delivering it someday in the summation of one of his trial cases.

Sarah was crestfallen. She thought, This is the type of sophomoric thinking that an expensive education brings a young person. And she shook her head in despair.

What followed was a very long period of silence. He realized he had made a mess of his argumentation in answer to Sarah's riddle, but for the life of him he didn't know what direction she was trying to lead him.

❄ ❄ ❄ ❄ ❄

In order to buy herself more time to think, she asked Michael to refresh her tea. He was glad for the break, and busied himself in the little kitchenette. When they were settled back down again, Sarah commenced an entirely new approach.

"The question before us, my young man, is this: what single thing do all human beings who have ever or will ever crawl upon the face of this earth have in common? Whether they are rich or poor, powerful or powerless, in the prime of health or on the verge of death, educated or uneducated, loved or abandoned. What, I say, what does every single human being have in common?"

Michael was getting very tired. It had been a long day and he felt his own bed calling. He looked at Sarah not without kindness and meekly said, " I don't know ' with a shrug of the shoulders.

"The answer to this question, Mr. Barron is the First Great Truth. A truth that once you realize and incorporate it into your heart, allows you to understand that all human beings are truly equal. The hatred, discrimination and racism that I lived through blazes forth as the ultimate of lies. When you realize this First Great Truth, you understand that regardless of your education or wealth or position, you are not one iota superior to anyone else. If you realize this truth and take it into your soul you will view all of humanity differently. It will change your life forever," she said, without the least bit of drama.

Michael stared hard at the old woman sitting in the bed. He was now fully awake and alert. For one of the few times in his life, he had nothing to say. It was it as if his heart had stopped in anticipation of a horrific crash that was a second away from occurring. His face alone spoke the question. "What is this truth?"

Sarah, satisfied that she had finally gained access to his mind, stated it simply.

The truth is, Michael, that no matter who we are, where we are in life, or what our condition is, we are all simply fellow travelers. Travelers who are marching, walking, crawling, dragging ourselves down the same road."

"Road?" He asked weakly. "We are all on the same road?"

Sarah said, very softly, like a mother speaking to her young child so as not to frighten him.

"Yes, my son. We are all on the same road…"

Michael didn't want to know the answer. For a second he debated running out of the room. The only sound was the ticking of the old clock on her bed stand, as these two human beings so different from one another, stared into each other's eyes. Finally, the young attorney asked meekly, "Where does this road lead?"

Again, she looked at him like a mother trying to comfort a frightened little child.

"To the Grave, my son, to the Grave."

CHAPTER SIX

Despite his extreme fatigue, he fell asleep only with the greatest difficulty that night. His discussion with Sarah had greatly disturbed him. On the one hand, he was inclined to dismiss it completely. After all, her so-called "First Great Truth" was so obvious it wasn't even worth mentioning. On the other hand, the more he tossed and turned in his bed and thought about it the more he realized it was like an onion, which she had carefully peeled, layer after layer, to reveal an ever more poignant truth.

As he tossed and turned he had begun to see that the crafty old lady was not talking about the obvious fact that we all die someday, no... She was making a much deeper point. The realization of the First Great Truth, the incorporation of this truth into one's very soul, would not just focus you on the important things of life. It would change your complete outlook on life.... and your fellow human beings. For if one fully realizes the implications of this truth, all discrimination and inequality, all artificial standards of social status, would disappear like the early morning fog over Chicago's lakefront.

He finally fell asleep with a much deeper appreciation of this old woman that Fate had thrown into his path. He was filled with curiosity as to what the other three "Great Truths" could possibly be.

When Michael woke a few hours later, he was surprisingly refreshed. More than that, he seemed to have clarity of vision he had not had in years. He got ready for work as quickly as he could, descended to street level, and stepped out into the cold winter air of the Midwestern United States.

This morning, I'll treat myself and take a taxi to work, he thought, with a smile on his face. His doorman hailed a cab and he soon found himself staring at the back of a turban-wrapped head. He announced his destination to the Indian cabdriver who responded with a chipper, "Very good, sir," and off they went.

As is the custom of cabbies all over the world, the cabdriver was the first to attempt light conversation. "Well, I suppose you are very busy this time of year, sir?" he said with a sharp British accent. Michael responded that he was busy most of the year. "I meant, sir, this is your Christmas season, is it not the time of your God's birth?"

Great, here we go, Michael thought. "Yeah, I guess you could say that."

The cabbie fearing that he might have given offense to his customer immediately attempted to clarify the situation.

"What I meant, sir, was that I have studied the Christian religion. I know about your three Gods, The Father, the Virgin Mother, and the Baby."

It was obvious that the cabbie was very proud of his erudition.

Well, at least he's trying. It's close enough, Michael thought.

"Yes, yes I know all about the three Gods. In my religion, we have many gods also."

Michael began to feel himself filling with contempt for this ignorant immigrant. But when he remembered Sarah's First Great Truth, the sarcastic response he had planned choked in his throat.

What right do I have to criticize this guy? Thought Michael. He's at least trying to understand my religion, whereas I could not even tell him the first thing about his. The young lawyer fell silent.

When they arrived at Michael's office building on Wacker Drive, he gave the cabbie an extra-large tip. As he exited to the street he looked him in the eye and wished him a very Merry Christmas. He chuckled out loud as he walked into the lobby of the building. It was the first time he had wished a stranger a 'Merry Christmas' in many a year. And a Hindu, no less!

❊ ❊ ❊ ❊ ❊

The day began faster than was normally the case. Michael Barron had a mountain of work to accomplish before the break for Christmas. This frenzied activity masked his emotions that day. But as the morning moved on, inexplicably, he became more and more depressed. His conversation of the night before was playing in the back of his mind like a worn-out tape recorder. Although the realization of the First Great Truth would certainly change how one viewed one's fellow human beings, it seemed to Michael that it couldn't help but also cast its possessor into the most profound depression. For the implication was, no matter what we did, no matter how hard we struggled… It was all in vain.

"Vanity, vanity, all is vanity." Sarah had quoted the Bible.

Michael worked straight through lunch for the schedule of the day called for the office party to begin at two p.m. This was usually a joyous occasion for everyone in the firm, not the least due to the fact that the annual bonus checks were handed out at this party. Promptly at two the celebration began. Michael still had much work to do, so he decided to come in tomorrow, on a Saturday, to work in his office alone. One was not late for this party.

As usual, the staff had done a great job in its decorations of the office. The refreshments were of the first quality, and the beverages included Michael's favorite champagne.

As Michael surveyed the office, he turned aside to his secretary Susan McDougal and said in a quiet whisper. " First class as always, Susan first class." She smiled an acknowledgment.

"And as always, Mr. Barron, I made your favorite." Michael forced a smile. He knew what was coming. Susan's ancestry was from the British Isles. She thought it was mandatory that everyone should enjoy Oyster Stew at Christmas tide. It was a very long-standing tradition (and recipe) in her family, and she assumed everyone in the firm would appreciate it. Michael didn't. He hated the stuff. But later on, when he watched the pleasure his secretary received from ladling out her family treasure into specially decorated Christmas cups while giving a hearty greeting of the season to each employee, he understood, rather, he accepted another implication of Sarah's truth… that the world was not all about him.

When it became time in the party for the speeches, Michael as a partner of the firm could not bypass the duty but his heart was not in it. The very festive atmosphere of the party seemed to make him more and more despondent.

What's the use? He thought. Sarah's right. Everyone in this room will someday be in their graves. And what will they have accomplished? When called upon, Michael made his speech, but his heart was not in it. His loyal assistant Joe Poleski watched him with growing concern. He knew something was not right with his boss.

Michael did his best to feign surprise when the president of his firm gave him his annual bonus check. He already knew the size of it, so it was just one more role that he had to play in this world. But his spirits were momentarily lifted as he saw the look of gratitude and surprise as each of his staff members opened their check.

I guess this is what it's all about, he thought.

As soon as it was seemly, he began to make his move toward exiting the party. He stated to everyone who would listen how much shopping he still had to do, how much preparation he had for the annual meeting, and that he would be coming in the office tomorrow morning on a Saturday to finish his work. It was all true, of course, except for the part about buying presents for his family and loved ones. He glanced over his shoulder at Susan, and for the first time was extremely jealous of his secretary. He may well have had the power, the money, the fame. But someone like Susan with her large family, her family traditions, and the simple joys she took in life… He now understood that on that long road they were both on, she would arrive at their mutual destination as one of life's true winners.

But as he rushed through the doors of the lobby of his office building that afternoon, two days before Christmas, he had already forgotten about the very large check in his pocket. A few days before such a financial windfall would have meant everything to him. Now he only wanted to be with his own family. He turned his steps towards a small basement apartment:

on the north side of Chicago.

CHAPTER SEVEN

Barron flipped the collar up on his expensive overcoat as he stepped briskly down the Chicago street. Moment by moment the heavy gray snow clouds appeared to be descending downward on the city. The early gloom of a Chicago December afternoon matched his mood perfectly. He glanced up at the lowering sky and thought, a white Christmas after all.

He deviated from his normal routine by turning suddenly south and then east. There was no real plan to his wanderings, but he felt he needed a little extra time to think things out. Slowly he passed into a seedier area of the loop. As with all of Chicago, he knew the neighborhood well. He was coming up to a soup kitchen, a place he normally avoided because it filled him with contempt.

"Losers, everyone's a loser," he would say to himself as he passed the Relief Center.

The mission was in an old abandoned store. The side facing the sidewalk was all glass. Through the shabby blinds one could easily see the men, and a few women, sitting at long picnic tables. It was a scene Michael had seen many times before. He was always amazed at the variety of human beings that occupied the center. Men and women of all ages and colors and, judging from their clothes, backgrounds. But they all had one thing in common. They were hungry, they were cold, and this was their last refuge.

As he drew parallel to the first set of windows of the mission, he noticed that it was more crowded than usual. Of course it never dawned on him that it was nearing the end of the month when many people run out of money and have no place to turn.

A few steps further and he came to a complete halt, turning to stare in the window. He froze in his tracks for not more than six feet from him on the other side of the plate glass stood the Salvation Army bell ringer, the girl he had seen in front of the church the day before. What was her name? Maria?

When he stopped she looked up and their eyes met. It was a moment that froze both of them. She was in the process of ladling out soup to the row of men who sat at the first table in front of the windows. Michael broke away his stare long enough to glance down into the bowl nearest him. The soup looked terrible, watery thin, in sharp contrast to the rich oyster stew, whose taste was still in his mouth. He glanced back up into Maria's eyes. The slight look of shocked recognition on her face was replaced by the most open, trusting, warm smile the young attorney had ever seen on anyone's face. She nodded her head in recognition to him, as she made a slight wave with the soup ladle in her hand. He broke into a forced smile, nodded his head, and turned to continue his walk past the front of the Mission.

"Boy, that's a coincidence," he said out loud, to no one.

When he reached the end of a long line of windows he paused again and turned to gaze once more inside the soup kitchen. Once again he stopped cold, for there sat a man that Michael recognized. He sat in the last seat next to the wall, wrapped in a dirty, frayed but expensive overcoat with a cheap sailor's cap pulled down over his head. His stubbled face was worn and haggard. He did not at first notice Michael, for he was completely absorbed in wolfing down the soup and bread.

Suddenly, the man felt the presence of Michael and jerked his head upward to look through the glass at his observer. The look of recognition on his face confirmed to Michael their previous acquaintance. The look on Michael's face spoke for itself.

The man looked down at his meager meal and began eating as fast as he could. As he did so his free hand went up to his sailor's cap and he pulled it down further in what appeared to be a vain attempt to cover his identity. He glanced up just once to see Michael still standing there in complete shock. He brought his hand down to cover his eyes as if the non-existent sun was shining directly into his face. And then, to Michael's horror, his whole body began to shake. He was sobbing. Sobbing with embarrassment, shame and humiliation. Barron turned on his heels and almost ran the rest of the way to his L stop.

Michael paused outside the door of Sarah's apartment. He had stopped on his way to her home at a corner grocery store to pick up what he thought would be much needed supplies: fresh bread, cold cuts, cans of hearty soup, fruit, which he now shifted in his arms so that he could lightly tap on her door.

The room looked exactly the way he had left it the night before, but Sarah didn't. She looked worse, much worse.

"The Calvary is here with fresh supplies," Michael announced with a loud voice and a smile on his face. But the old woman only nodded her head in weak acknowledgment. He busied himself putting away the groceries.

"And how are we feeling today?" He asked her, while feigning cheerfulness. She didn't answer immediately.

Finally, she responded. "Sit down Michael," she ordered, "we have much work to do this night."

"Sure, sure," he said, attempting to humor her. "But first we must eat!" Michael began preparing a meal. Sarah simply watched him but didn't respond.

Michael prepared a simple but hearty meal of sandwiches, soup and sliced fruit. He helped her sit up in her bed and placed one dinner tray across her lap while he sat down in his customary rocking chair with a second tray on his knees. For some reason he was ravenous but he noticed Sarah hardly touched her food.

As he ate his dinner, he attempted to formulate the argument he would use for Sarah to convince her to go to the hospital. But as usual, she was way ahead of him.

She cut off his train of thought by asking him "Well, my young friend. Have you thought about our discussions of last night?"

The slight degree of cheerfulness he had been able to attain since he entered Sarah's apartment dissipated when he thought of the reflections he had gone through the night before.

"Yeah, I thought about it, but it's not exactly a cheery topic for the holiday season."

In a split-second Sarah was fully awake and focused on her young visitor. "How so?" she asked in a clear attempt on her part to draw Michael out further. He thought to himself that this crafty woman was not interested in his words, merely his attitude.

"Well, it's rather obvious isn't it"? He finally stated between mouthfuls of food. "Obviously we're all going to die someday. Therefore, as you would put it we are all on the same road to the same place. But to me, what's interesting are the implications one should draw from this," he stated in his best professorial voice, as if the old lady could never have thought this through.

"Oh," she replied, failing to resist a smile as it spread across her face.

Michael paused when he glanced at her sideways and was more than a little annoyed as he realized that this uneducated woman was light-years ahead of him.

He tried to recover. "Yes, anyone could see immediately the implications of your First Great Truth."

"How so?" She continued to play with him.

Taking a rest from his eating he leaned back even further in the old rocker. Pressing his fingertips together in the attitude of the most learned of his profession, he began in a condescending manner.

"Well, even a child could see the 'prima facie' conclusions of this First Great Truth of yours."

"Please explain it to me." She said with her most disarming smile.

This woman can really be a annoying, Michael thought, but he continued. "Obviously," he stated, "if we are all on the same road, if we are just fellow travelers to the grave, and there are no real differences between any of us in terms of race, religion, culture, values, beliefs, well then, utilizing your view of the human condition, such things obviously form no basis for any distinction between people."

Sarah said. "Very well stated Mr. Barron, I can see why you are a leading practitioner of your profession.

Michael knew he was being played with, he just didn't know how much.

"But I would be interested to know, since we are discussing this subject, what if any conclusions you draw from my little truth." Her eyes focused like a laser on the young man.

He thought, now the ball is on my side of the court. I'll show this woman what sound logical reasoning is really like! It was not for nothing that Michael Barron was considered the best litigator of his firm. As he paused for dramatic effect, he began rocking slowly in the old chair, struck his most contemplative yet professional pose, and collected his thoughts for his rebuttal. His legally trained mind, quickly listed the possible objections and rebuttals, carefully weighing each one. And then he began his reply.

" Certainly your views, Sarah,have merit, but one must consider, one must understand that things are not just black and white. You must see that there are many ways one could respond to this First Great Truth of yours."

But then he made the mistake of looking directly into her eyes. The objections and rebuttals he had formulated with such certitude turned to ashes. He fell silent. He attempted to start eating again, but he had lost his appetite. He knew Sarah was right, and he also knew that if he accepted the full implication of the First Great Truth, much of his life , perhaps all of his life, had been built…

On a lie.

CHAPTER EIGHT

They finished their meal in silence. Occasionally, Michael glanced up to look at Sarah. He felt like a butterfly being studied under a magnifying glass. He didn't like the feeling. So he made another attempt to take command of the situation.

He failed again and lapsed into silence. His previous self-assurance, his arrogance, had finally dissipated. The very attitude of his body changed in the old rocker. Sarah saw this and her attitude also changed towards her young visitor. The door was open to his heart, she had waited for this. She thought, Thank God. Now we can make some progress! She decided to push the door open and walk in directly. "You are very astute, Mr. Barron," Sarah began, with all the sincerity she could muster.

He looked up at her. "How so?" He asked, with sarcasm in his voice.

"You have already deduced much of the lessons of the First Great Truth. Obviously, if we are every day closer to our final destination of the graveyard, we will, in the words of one philosopher, 'live each day as if it were our last'."

"Carpe Diem, eh?" Michael asked, half-heartedly.

"Precisely so. And you quickly deduced what many people would not see. That is the rather obvious fact now that if the First Great Truth is correct, all discrimination, all racial hatred, all artificial distinctions made between human beings are ridiculous."

"And if carried to their ultimate extreme, as you saw during the war, discrimination leads to the ultimate in evil and obscenity!" Michael added, warming to the discussion.

Sarah nodded her head ever so slightly. After what seemed like an eternity, the old woman finally said, "Are there any further conclusions we can draw from this Great Truth?"

For once, Michael was keeping up with her. "Such as?" He asked.

"Well, that if all of this is true, would it not appear to be the case that all human life, indeed all life, is precious, and if we accept this as a corollary, would it not logically follow that all life should be preserved and nurtured by us so-called intelligent human beings?" Sarah's question hung in the air between them.

"Well," said Michael, immediately perceiving where Sarah was going with these arguments, "this would get us into much more complicated topics than we could possibly discuss tonight." He chuckled, "You know, capital punishment, abortion, euthanasia, subjects that must be well thought out, and their conclusions carried out, no matter how distasteful they may be."

"Yes, I saw some of these conclusions carried out, in Germany."

Michael flushed beet-red, and then decided to change the subject by taking a little break. He stood up to stretch his legs, but quickly realized there was little place for him to go in such a small apartment. He walked over to the small window near the ceiling that looked out upon the street. Through the security bars, he could see the snow falling gently on the uneven sidewalk in front of Sarah's building. The streetlights gave just enough light for him to gaze upon this cityscape. For some reason the view that evening made this little apartment seem all the more comfortable.

"More tea?" He finally asked, speaking over his shoulder. "Yes, please," she responded, and he was happy to have something to do. He was amazed at how attached he had become to this old woman, as radically different as they both were from each other, in just the last few days.

He served the tea and sat down again to continue their discussion.

"What you say may well be true, Miss Silberstein, but as far as I can see, you've missed the most important inference from this Great Truth of yours."

"Oh?"

"Well yes," he responded. "The conclusions you draw from this First Great Truth are the positive consequences, but there is a much more negative side, a darker side to your truth." Sarah stared at him intently, and Michael was pleased that he now had her full attention. "As I see it, the full ramifications of your Great Truth are incredibly depressing."

Sarah didn't respond, so he continued. "You see if what you say is true, the other side of the coin is that no matter what we do, no matter how hard we try, no matter what we accomplish in our lives, it's all for naught.

If the beggar and the King, the common soldier and the general, all wind up in the same graveyard, what difference does any of it make? By the time you have struggled all of your life to accomplish some of your goals, to make a name for yourself, to accumulate some capital…Well, you are just that much closer to dust and ashes.

"And if you are one of the unfortunate ones of this world," the lawyer continued, "you grow up, live and die in poverty and ignorance, or you struggle through great evil, like you had to do, Sarah, as a young girl... How can there be any redeeming value to this life?"

Michael looked away, lost in thought, "But it goes even further," he said. Sarah could see his mind searching and stretching, analyzing. "Yes, yes it goes even further, if there is a God, if there is a Creator of this world, why has he not terminated this human foolishness? Even more," Michael grew agitated. "Even more, when the Creator views the history, the sorry history of his human creations on this planet, how could he possibly allow this to continue?"

Michael returned his gaze to Sarah, and he said, "After the evil you've seen, surely you must be despondent. You must be depressed over the human condition!"

If it were possible, the intent look on Sarah's face became even more focused. "Would you kindly hand me the third book from the left on the bookshelf above my writing desk?" Michael went to retrieve the book and realized with a start it was the Christian Bible. When he picked it up he could not help but notice how dog-eared and worn the book was. He handed the book to her with a comical look on his face.

She read his thoughts. "Do you find it amusing that I read your Bible?"

"Well..." he said. He couldn't finish his thought. Sarah just chuckled.

She opened the much read book and thumbed through it until she found the passages she wanted and then without fanfare, she began to read out loud:

Vanity, vanity, all things are vanity
What profit has a man from all the labor, which he toils
at under the sun?
One generation passes and another comes, but the
world forever stays
All speech is labored. There is nothing man can say
The eye is not satisfied with seeing, nor is there the ear
filled with hearing
What has been that will be, what has been done, that
will be done. Nothing is new under the sun. Even things
which we say, 'this is new,' has already existed in the
ages that preceded us.
There is no remembrance of the men of old, nor of
those to come will there be any remembrance among
those who come after them.

Ecclesiastes 1:2-11

Michael jumped up from his chair, "Exactly! Exactly! That's just what I was thinking! So what's the use?" He started pacing around the little room in agitation.

"Please sit down, Michael," she said. He obeyed like a young child. He thought of leaving. He didn't want to, but the discussion had made him more depressed than he'd ever been in his entire life. It was almost Christmas, another year gone, and what did he have to show for it? True, he had money, political power, prestige. But what had it gotten him two days before Christmas? He thought, my employees have their families to go home to, their plans to make for Christmas morning. But me, here I sit in the squalor of a basement apartment in a less than desirable old neighborhood of an old city, debating with a poor immigrant woman who has nothing to show for her life either.

Yes, he was more depressed than he had ever been in his life. He began to summon his strength to stand up and begin his cold winter's walk back to his luxurious, but empty, condominium. He slowly stood up and looked at Sarah. As always she was reading his thoughts almost as quickly as he had them. She didn't try to stop him from leaving. She just transfixed his eyes with that peculiar, intense stare of hers. He was the first to speak.

"Well," he began, "I guess it's time for me to -" He couldn't finish the sentence, he needed to leave, but he knew he really had no place to go.

"This is it," she said softly.

He was frightened to his core by what he was afraid the old woman was going to say next.

"This is it," she softly said, again, "what you have been searching for. The turning point of your life."

At any other time, at any other place, he would've broken into

60

laughter. Instead, he made the decision to stay and collapsed heavily into the old rocker. A smile of approbation slowly spread across the old gentle woman's face. "I knew I had made the right decision. You are the one!"

"The one? The one for what?" His entire attitude, his entire body spoke of his fatigue and depression. At that moment he wouldn't have lifted his own hand an inch to save his own life. He looked up at Sarah. She spoke in the most kindly and motherly way.

"Yes" she said to no one in particular. "You are finally ready."

"Ready for what?" he responded warily.

She reached out to hold his hand as if to transmit her strength and her courage into him. She finally said:

"The Second Great Truth."

PART THE THIRD

CHAPTER NINE

Fearful they shall come,
At the counting up of their sins,
And their lawless deeds,
Shall convict them to their face.
Wisdom 4: 20

Sarah had nodded off asleep, she looked every bit her age and her recent trauma had weakened her, frighteningly so. Michael took the opportunity to stretch his legs and more closely examine the content of the little apartment that snowy evening on the northside of Chicago.

He picked up the well-worn Bible from which Sarah had been quoting. He noticed in her minute handwriting she had annotated page after page. Some of the notes he understood. Some were a complete mystery to him, but as he flipped through the Bible he noticed that some of the passages had been marked in red ink with numerals. Some had been numbered one, some two or three. He noticed that the passage that Sarah had read to him was marked with a large number one. He placed the Bible carefully back on her lap and proceeded to examine the rest of her library. The contents seem to center around philosophy, theology and history. None of it was light reading. One volume, he recognized from his college days: *The Meditations* by Renée Descartes. He opened the cover and noticed that every square inch on the inside covers, in the margin of the pages, on the back inside cover, was filled with Sarah's notes in her cramped, minute handwriting.

Boy, he thought, she just doesn't read a book, she studies it. He glanced back at her when he heard a prodigious snore. He turned around slowly, and gazed out the small basement window at the snow lightly falling through the amber light of the streetlamp. Once again Michael thought, What am I doing here? He poured himself another mug of tea and sat down in the rocker next to Sarah's bed. His mind began to drift over his life.

The contrast between Michael and Sarah's lives could not have been greater. He truly had been born with a silver spoon in his mouth. The only son of well-to-do physicians, he grew up in Lake Forest, Illinois. He enjoyed every privilege and opportunity. The very best college preparatory elementary and high schools had provided his schooling. Then it was on to Yale and back to Northwestern for law school. His life during those years had been one of country clubs and tennis courts during the summer, squash courts, and fraternity activities during the school year, with as much foreign travel squeezed in as his academic studies would allow.

He tried to imagine what Sarah's youth must have been like in

Poland, but he failed miserably. The contrast was just too great. A crack appeared in his arrogance as he reflected how he might have turned out, had he been born into Sarah's family at that period in history.

What amazed him most, however, was how people like Sarah could possibly be so intelligent. He had always assumed that intelligence was a mixture of nature and nurture. Not only did you have to be born with the right genes, but also you had to come from the right family environment to have a high intelligence. Which is why Michael J. Barron, Esquire had always cast a wary eye on scholarships granted to the poorest of the poor.

He returned to his reflections on his own past. During law school he had met a female law student, who, like him, had lived a life of privilege. Every one of his family and friends thought it was a perfect match. Her family background, the ease with which she walked through the highest social circles of life; no one doubted that this would be a good match for the up-and-coming young attorney.

Michael chuckled. In fact it was a complete disaster of a marriage for in his youthful ignorance he had married someone just like himself. Such people have a hard time living with themselves, much less with a clone, and within a few years it was over. The young attorney had taken such a beating in the divorce court of Cook County, Illinois that he vowed never to marry again.

And so he devoted himself to his work, building a solid edifice based on his legal accomplishments, his drive, his thirst for power and of course, money. Well, at least I haven't done too badly on that score, he thought, as he padded his breast pocket with the magnificent bonus check folded neatly inside. But then he turned and looked at Sarah.

Sarah awoke with a loud snort. It took her a few seconds to regain her orientation. She sat up in her bed and began to apologize. "Oh, my goodness! You'll have to forgive an old lady. It seems I took a little catnap there."

"Quite all right, Sarah," he responded. "I've been enjoying your library. You have quite eclectic tastes."

"Well, I wouldn't call my taste eclectic." She rubbed the sleep from her eyes. "Most of my books center on just a few subjects."

"Yes, I noticed that… mostly philosophy, theology and history."

"Precisely so! You see, Michael, I have been searching-" But she stopped in mid-sentence, as if she were reluctant to reveal too much about herself.

Michael saw his opportunity to learn more about this remarkable gentlewoman. "Would it be too painful for you to tell me more about how you came into possession of these Four Great Truths? You mentioned that a Catholic priest taught you these concepts while you were in the camps of World War II. But where did he get them from?"

The old lady's eyes narrowed, "Well done, counselor! You drove right to the heart of the matter. You obviously connected the dots between my fields of study and these Four Great Truths."

"Well, it was somewhat obvious." Michael responded arrogantly, in an offhand manner.

"I understand, I understand," she acknowledged. "It's only natural to wonder about such a thing."

Michael could see she was allowing her mind to drift back many years. A great sadness came over her. After a long pause, she finally said, "It is impossible to describe the horror of those days. As I look back, after so many years have passed, it is as if another person, not me, had lived through that torture." She paused to take a long drink from her strong tea as if to give herself strength. "You see Michael in those years I had the misfortune of being born with two strikes against me. The first was that I was a Polish Jew. But the second turned out to be equally dangerous. I was born an identical twin. When the Gestapo and the Einstaz groupen began their roundup of Jews throughout the so-called eastern territories, my family fell into their clutches. I quickly lost contact with everyone but my sister. My family, even to this day, I do not know what happened to them. They kept my sister and me together just because we were twins.

"As I mentioned before, we eventually wound up at this large collection of concentration camps, known as Auschwitz. The Nazis of course did not tell us the truth. No, no, they were too smart for that. They told us that work would make us free. We were so naïve we believed them, and each of us did his/her appointed tasks at the various factories in and around Auschwitz. They used to use the women for the delicate work of assembling fuses for artillery shells. The rations were so poor, our clothes so inadequate, that there were many days where we thought death would be a blessing. We had no idea what was to come.

"It wasn't long before we came to the attention of this doctor that I've told you about. We nicknamed him the Angel of Death. What he did, even today, I cannot speak of. It was beyond all human comprehension. He called it his medical experiments. I understand the pig survived the war and is hiding in South America. I do not believe in violence Michael, but I tell you, there are thousands of human beings alive today that if they could get their hands on this man..." She trailed off.

"This so-called doctor was medically interested in the biology of twins, and so in due course my sister and I were given over to his gentle custody."

Michael interrupted her as he could see she was about to explode in tears. "That's enough, Sarah," he said, "you don't have to go any further."

"No," she said firmly. "I have talked about this earlier, and you need to know the truth." Sarah took a sip of her tea. "So my sister and I were used as guinea pigs for his so-called genetic research." She paused for the longest time, and then obviously thought better of continuing. "Suffice to say, Michael, my sister died of her injuries. I somehow survived, but of course was never able to start my own family. The doctor lost interest in me. So the General Administration of the camps decided to use me to provide aid and comfort for their soldiers." She started to choke up and could not go on.

Michael remembering the tattoo on her arm, said firmly. "Thank you Sarah, that's enough. Let's talk about something else."

Throughout the conversation, neither of this strange couple noticed the sad face staring at them through the little basement window.

A white haired man with dark glasses.

69

CHAPTER TEN

"No, she said firmly, you have asked me for the facts once again, and I will give them to you. Besides, you need to know the truth for your-" She didn't finish the sentence. "I have mentioned to you this Catholic priest before, how he was executed by the SS, how he gave us hope in our darkest hours. He was truly one of the 'Righteous Ones.' Even to this day, Michael, it pains me greatly to think of him. You are the first person in a long, long time, to whom I have mentioned this man.

"You see many people were swept up in what today we call the Holocaust. The world is beginning to understand what happened to the Jewish people but it didn't stop there, Michael. The handicapped, the homosexuals, the Gypsies, anyone these Nazi criminals thought was significantly below them in the hierarchy of their racial follies, and of course, everyone they referred to as 'partisans.' This meant anyone who in anyway opposed the Nazi government, including the Christian clergy. For example at Auschwitz, there was a complete camp, a village that was reserved just for Gypsies. The so-called SS scientists studied them until they were chosen for liquidation. The SS referred to it as special treatment. You and I would call it mass murder.

"Well, this righteous Catholic priest that I refer to, he was arrested for being a partisan because he voiced critical comments of the Nazi regime. His kind, gentle and understanding nature caused him to be well received by all, even some of the SS guards. I think it was because of this that he was allowed more freedom of movement in the camps than normal prisoners.

"But one day, even his time ran out. I'm sure Michael, you've heard of the gassing chambers, the crematories. Of that hell on earth. But thousands more were executed at a special place inside the center of the camp. It was a long brick wall with telephone poles inserted in the ground in front of it. The prisoners that were selected for 'special treatment' would be marched through the center of the camp to that brick wall and there, by the simple method of firing squad, liquidated. I saw it happen to this just man, this priest, who did so much to help everyone in the camp. All these decades later, Michael, I can see him standing in front of the wall, facing his executioners at the moment before the order was given. I cannot describe the look on his face. It was one of pity, and sorrow, but not for himself, Michael, not for himself. It was for his executioners, these young men, 17, 18 years of age of the Totenkopf division of the SS. These young men, about to pull the trigger, were so unsettled by his stare, they fired erratically when the order was given." The old woman burst into tears.

Michael tactfully decided it was time for a break. "Well Sarah," he said cheerfully, "I think I'll have some of this fine chicken noodle soup, would you like some?"

She shook her head no between the sobs.

"Good, that's just the ticket for both of us!" He ignored her. This gave him a much-needed chance for both of them to compose themselves as he busied himself making the second part of their meal.

When he sat down again to serve the soup, Sarah pointed to her old overcoat hanging on a hook behind the door. She motioned for Michael to bring it to her. He put his bowl of soup down and did so. He thought she had asked for the coat because she was cold. But instead, when he spread it out on top of her on the bed, she pointed to a lapel pan. It was a small chip of wood with a safety pin on one side of it and on the other what looked like a wilted sprig of an evergreen tree branch, stapled through the wood. Apparently it was Sarah's idea of a Christmas ornament.

She lightly touched the evergreen ornament and told Michael that this priest had given it to her. So very long ago, the priest had explained to the young Sarah that the evergreen was the one plant that thrived in the hottest of weather and coldest winters, the one plant that never lost its greenery and was able to bring a little cheer in the darkest of winter nights. Its branches sheltered wildlife of all sorts. She looked at Michael as if to ask: Do you understand what he was saying?

Michael didn't, but he gave a slight nod anyway.

"I've worn this little pin every holiday season since," Sarah continued, "to remind me of my-" She left the rest unsaid.

"Very interesting," he said, feigning an insight into the symbolic importance of the ornament, "but I believe you were going to tell me tonight about your Second Great Truth."

Sarah looked at him, startled. "But I am." Then she looked away and frowned as if to say, I wonder if this young man is learning anything.

They finished their simple meal in silence. He could see Sarah's mind working furiously. She would occasionally glance at him and then quickly glance back at the little window to the snowy street outside. Obviously, she was trying to decide how to proceed on an entirely new subject.

Finally, she began. "You mention Michael that one of the things you came away with from your contemplation of the First Great Truth was a deep and overwhelming sense of despair, not just for yourself, but for all humankind."

"Yeah, I guess that's right."

"You were right to do so, that is certainly one of the implications of this truth, and the long story of humankind reinforces this. Perhaps the greatest consequence of the realization of this truth is a sense of that abandonment. Not just for ourselves, but for all of our fellow travelers."

Michael jumped upright in his chair. "Exactly so! This First Great Truth does cause one to be completely focused, to enjoy each day as if it were his last, to treat all fellow human beings as he would wish to be treated. But that, ultimately, we are all alone in this world with nothing but grief, sickness, decay, old age, and finally the graveyard to look forward to." The lawyer slumped down into his chair in despondency.

Sarah's expression visibly brightened. "I see you've thought this through carefully," she said with a certain degree of satisfaction in her voice.

Michael grunted his response instead of speaking.

"And you are right." Sarah said. "This would be the summation of human existence on this planet. If all there was, was the First Great Truth!"

Sarah struggled to sit up in her bed. "I want to sit up in the armed chair in the corner, my boy. Please give me a hand." Michael helped the old woman into the chair.

"Pull your rocker up over here."

The two sat with their knees almost touching each other. Sarah made several false starts, and then stopped. Clearly she had something of great import to say to this young man. But she didn't know how to begin.

"Michael," she finally said, "do you believe in God?"

He looked at her and shrugged his shoulders. "Well, I guess I do, but I often wonder."

"And so does everyone Michael. So does everyone. But, if we logically examine the alternative that an atheist would have us believe, that the 100 and some basic elements of this universe were put into some sort of mixer and stirred well, and that with enough time, the incomprehensible majesty of this universe simply evolved. Does this seem like a logical and physical possibility to you?"

"I don't know."

Sarah realized that this line of conversation would take them way too far a field.

"Would you be willing to acknowledge that there is some form of life, some form of intelligence, which I believe the famous science Albert Einstein referred to as the 'Mysterious?' Something or someone, some intelligence that created, organized, and animated the entire universe?"

Michael thought for a moment and then replied, "I guess so."

"Fine, let us agree to call this force the 'Spiritus Mundi,' the spirit of the world."

"Okay. But are you claiming there is only one Spiritus Mundi, one God?"

Sarah nodded.

"Why then," asked Michael, again warming to the occasion, "is there no majority opinion concerning this God? Why then have so many segments of humanity had so many differing opinions as to the nature, appearance, and ways of worshiping this God?"

Sarah responded. "When you were growing up Michael, did you have a favorite relative? An uncle or aunt? A grandfather, perhaps?"

"Well, yes. I had an uncle."

Sarah asked if his uncle was married and if he had children.

"Yes. Three."

Sarah smiled. "Do you suppose that his wife would view him and know him in one way, his own brothers and sisters in another? His parents in yet another. His children in yet another. And you, perhaps his favorite nephew, would your view of him not be unique?"

Michael nodded his assent.

"And if you brought all the people that ever knew him into one room and ask them to describe him, would their descriptions not vary greatly? Their understanding of him, their memories of him. Their assessment of his capabilities, would all these opinions not vary greatly from person to person who knew this uncle of yours?"

Michael smiled despite himself.

"Agreed," he said, "but you have to admit, the things mankind has done in the name of God is enough to turn anyone against religion."

"You are confusing God and his worship with religion," Sarah said.

Michael chuckled, and his smile broadened. This old lady is amazing, he thought. He thought for a moment, and then he stated, "Well, be all this as it may, we were going to discuss your Second Great Truth."

"Quite so," she responded, turning very sober.

There was an awkward silence between them. Michael could sense she had no idea how to start this conversation. It was as if the dam was about to burst, but he didn't know how or where the first crack would appear. Finally, her gaze settled on the old Bible. She picked it up and read:

"Why is life given to the toilers,

And life to the bitter in spirit?

They wait for death that comes not;

they search for it rather than for hidden treasures.

Rejoice in it exultingly.

And are glad when they reach the grave."

Job 3: 20-22

"You see Michael the first truth serves two real purposes. First, it focuses our attention on what's important in this world and how we should view our fellow travelers. But secondly, if we think clearly on the subject we see the world realistically, we understand, that especially for the agnostic and atheist, there is no future. There is no comfort. There is no reassurance, no validation of our existence on this planet. And if we think clearly and correctly about this, we understand that despite all the pleasures this world has to offer, the end result is what you have encountered."

Michael did not interrupt her.

Sarah looked at him and said one word:

"Despair."

CHAPTER ELEVEN

Sarah asked to be helped back to her bed and as soon as she had made herself comfortable, she drifted off. Michael glanced at the clock. It was going on ten pm, and he thought he ought to get going. He walked over to the small window and looked out. There was very little traffic this Friday night before Christmas. The snow had accumulated to several inches on the sidewalk. He watched the flakes lazily float past the streetlamp to the pavement. His mind drifted many blocks away to his luxury condominium on the shore of Lake Michigan. He looked around Sarah's small apartment.

"What a difference!" He said aloud. He couldn't help but compare the exquisite furnishings of his condominium with the castoffs from Goodwill industries of Sarah's apartment. Sarah had virtually nothing except the bare essentials for survival in this little one-room apartment. He on the other hand had every modern convenience at his fingertips in his high-rise condominium. "Yes, he continued his thought. It's night and day between these two apartments… this one is a home!" Michael sat down in the armchair internally building the strength he would need to reenter the cold and walk the many blocks to his condominium. But the gurgle of the old steam radiator, the spiritual warmth of this little apartment soon overwhelmed him . And as he fell asleep in the old armchair he recalled what Sarah had said was the greatest form of suffering …loneliness.

This time it was Sarah who woke first from the catnap. "Michael," she called out, and he awoke with a start. He rubbed his eyes, sat up straight and glanced again at the clock. An hour-and-a-half had gone by. It was almost midnight.

Neither one wanted to acknowledge how late it was. Neither one wanted to lose the company of the other. There was something about this season of the year that made strangers want to cling to each other as they waited out the long, dark, snowy nights.

"So what you're saying Sarah," he began as if there had been no interruption, "is that the Second Great Truth is an antidote for the first?"

"Excellent counselor," she responded cheerfully, with just the slightest touch of sarcasm in her voice. "The Second Great Truth is the antidote to the despair, despondency and lack of hope, brought on by our contemplation of the First Great Truth."

"Pray go on," he said with mock seriousness. These two people so radically different from each other were beginning to find each other invaluable company for their otherwise empty lives.

She was once again sharp as a tack, and she quickly chose a course upon which to proceed. "Have you ever seen a baby born, Michael?"

He stared at her with slight disbelief at the turn in the conversation.

He finally responded no.

"Well, I have. First in the camps - you'd be surprised how many babies were born there - and then in my career as an aide working in hospitals. All of my life I have many times been pressed into service in that joyous capacity. Did you know Michael, that whenever a baby is born, the people who see it, the people who are there, they cry?"

Michael did not know what to say.

She chuckled to herself. "It's true. I've even seen very experienced obstetricians tear up at the birth of a baby. You expect it from the parents, but not from staff, and of course, the baby gets a little nudge from the doctor and out comes the wail and then the tears really flow. Tears of happiness, Michael, happiness."

Michael acknowledged that this must be so.

"There is a reason for this. Can you guess what it is?"

He shook his head no.

"Up until recently, Michael, death was much more common as an everyday experience than it is now, therefore all new life was treasured by the human species. It is my belief that all human beings retain this collective memory, which is what makes births so joyous. But there is another reason, a much more important reason for the tears.

"Every time a baby is born on this planet, regardless of the color of its skin, its religion, its family's wealth, or even if the baby is wanted by its parents, it is a sign from the Creator that we all have one more chance.

"It's an affirmation, Michael, an affirmation from the Spiritus

Mundi, from the Creator, that he, she or it has not given up on us, that we all have one more chance to get it right, despite our sorry history as a species. Do you understand how important this is Michael?"

He said yes, but he really did not understand.

Sarah smiled inwardly. She knew this young man had not seen the death and suffering that she had seen: therefore to him new life was plentiful. Indeed too much life was, in his opinion, just an annoyance.

He'll learn, she thought, with great sadness.

Finally, Michael responded, "One more chance for what?"

"To be what we were created to be!" The old woman responded with great force. "Think, Michael, think!" With great difficulty, she pulled herself up, as far as she could in her bed and asked for a glass of water.

After Michael brought the water, and Sarah regained her composure, she said, as way of explanation, "My son, you are here, we are here, for a reason!"

Michael was stunned into silence.

"Every new birth is to remind us of this universal truth and to deliver the message that you, we, all have one more chance, one more chance to be what we were intended to be. One more chance to fulfill our individual destinies. One more chance to get it right. Every new day we have choices, and those choices are ours, ours alone."

She fell back, exhausted from the explanation. After a moment Michael asked kindly, "Is this the Second Great Truth you have spoken of?"

"In part." She replied. "You see, every baby brings a message with it into this world. Two thousand years ago such a baby was born. He was a Jew born to parents so poor that the husband was unable to persuade the innkeeper to make room for his pregnant betrothed on the night of her delivery. Instead, she was forced to give birth in a cave, a cave that served as a barn. Despite these circumstances, this young baby grew up to become a great teacher, a rabbi, who spoke such words that the rich and powerful of this world could not tolerate him, and he was executed as a common criminal." The old woman paused to get her strength again.

"So, the Second Great Truth is that no matter what your religion, your beliefs, your circumstances you find yourself in this world of ours, you can believe in the message that this baby brought to the world so long ago. The same message that every new birth brings to the world."

Here it comes, Michael thought, a lecture on Christianity. I never thought this old Jewish woman would be a closet Christian.

"Yes, yes," he said impatiently. "I know, the baby was born to forgive all our sins. To atone for man's original sin, etcetera."

"Don't put words in my mouth, young man!" Sarah flashed with anger. "I did not say that." She inhaled deeply. "Nor for that matter, do I deny it. Such matters are for each individual to decide."

Michael stammered out an apology.

"No matter what you may believe of this Jewish baby," she continued after she had calmed down, "whether he was a great teacher, a great rabbi, a prophet, or divine, you must admit that no one had spoken like this young man had before.

"You see, Michael, all the great thinkers of the world made their own individual contributions. Aristotle taught logic. Plato, the primacy of ideas, Buddha, the focus on the importance of enlightenment. But this Jewish carpenter taught unconditional love for one's fellow human beings."

"So this is the essence of the Second Great Truth?" The weary lawyer asked.

"No, something even more important. The Second Great Truth teaches us that every baby, and especially that baby born 2000 years ago, gives all of us the greatest gift we human beings could possibly receive."

Michael sat up, erect, interested.

"You see young man, this baby whose birth we are about to celebrate, gave us all a very special Christmas gift. The gift of…

"Hope"

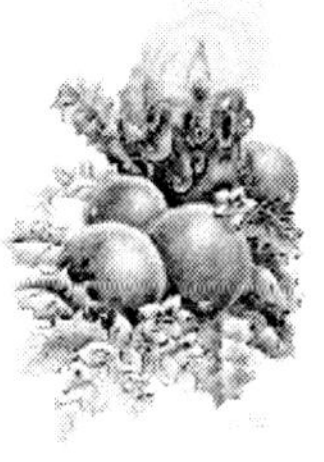

PART THE FOURTH

CHAPTER TWELVE

Coming events cast their shadows before

Cicero

Michael Barron turned up the collar of his overcoat and stepped into the cold night air. It was past midnight and the snow flurries had finally stopped. He turned towards the lake and thought he would walk at least some of the way back to his condominium before he hailed a taxi. But there was very little traffic out at that hour in the Christmas season and the thought occurred to him he might have to walk the entire way.

"Well, the exercise will do me good, and I won't have to worry about any muggers in this weather!" He chuckled. He had waited till Sarah had fallen into a deep sleep before leaving. His head swam with the thoughts she had put into it. He was confused, disoriented in spirit, by it all. The long walk would give him a chance to sort out his thoughts and feelings.

The colder air and exercise served as an antidote to the overheated little apartment, which he had just left. Despite the lateness of the hour, his mind felt razor-sharp. After a few moments reflection, he mumbled to himself, "What's most amazing is how these two Great Truths appear to be so simplistic, on the surface at least. But the more one thinks about it the more the ramifications flow forth. Obviously, everyone dies. Obviously, everyone takes the birth of baby as a sign of hope. Hope for the future." His mind was literally overwhelmed with the implications that followed from these simplistic facts.

He began to realize that these truths were nothing more than prisms by which one can view of the world in a completely new way. He didn't like what he saw. Not because it wasn't beautiful. Not because it wasn't eminently useful, but because it forced one to change one's view of the world, and more importantly, of one's self.

As he walked he mulled over the events of the last few days. If a few days ago someone had told him all that was about to transpire, he would have laughed in their face. A few days ago he had the universe figured out; a few days ago he had all the answers; a few days ago, he knew the truth about this old world. Michael thought, What a fool I was!

But fate, or something, had thrown this woman into his life. One part of him wished that he had never met her. Another part of him, despite the shortness of their acquaintance, could not imagine his life without her. He picked up his pace down the empty sidewalks of the North Side of Chicago. For some inexplicable reason, he wanted to cry.

After walking several more blocks Michael gained the intersection of the major north-south thoroughfare and Sarah's street. On the northwest corner of this intersection there stood a greasy- spoon, all-night restaurant that Michael had passed often. He was freezing, and perhaps due the hour his hunger was ravishing. Both sides of the restaurant were lined with glass windows and he could see clearly that several tables and booths were vacant. He decided to enter the swinging glass doors at the corner, and then assumed a seat in a booth by the window next to the cash register. Once in a while, he actually enjoyed eating in such a restaurant for he felt like he was one of the boys, dining with the "great unwashed masses." Of course he knew nothing could be further from the truth. He glanced over the specials written on a blackboard propped near the entrance. A 300-pound waiter cum manager came over with pencil and order book in hand.

"What'll it be tonight, Mac?" He asked.

Michael picked the first item he could see: a large bowl of five-alarm chili, crackers and a drink. He already had a bit of indigestion, from his unusual supper at Sarah's apartment, so he thought "What the hell? I might as well go out in style tonight."

"I'll take the chili," he said, "and a glass of milk." The bald waiter grunted, turned on his heels and headed back behind the counter. He glanced over at the counter and through the reflecting glass on the wall he studied the faces of the men; there were no women. In the past, he would have seen just a group of losers. But now as he carefully looked at each one, he could tell they all had a story to tell. They were late-night workers, cabdrivers, guys getting off the PM shift from somewhere. No one said a word to each other. They ate their meals in silence.

His reflection on this cross segment of humanity was interrupted by the arrival of the largest bowl of chili he'd ever seen, a basket of bread and crackers and a tall glass of milk.

"Is that it, Mac?" The waiter asked.

"Yeah, thanks," Michael dug into the meal with relish. He had forgotten how good a simple bowl of homemade chili could be in a simple restaurant like this. As he glanced out the window south, down the great avenue towards the loop, he saw that hardly anybody was out. Very few vehicles cruised the boulevard. A man who had been sitting at the far end of the counter rose and quickly exited through the front door. Michael paid no attention until he heard the waiter swear.

"I knew it! I knew that weird old guy would stiff me!" The waiter rushed to the end of the counter to see what money the white-haired man with dark glasses had left under his bill. When he lifted up the check, he spied a coin. Michael turned to observe the scene.

The waiter said out loud to no one. "What the hell is this?" He walked slowly back to the cash register to examine the coin that lay under the check more fully in the brighter light of the entrance of the restaurant.

Michael glanced up at him and said, "Let me have a look at it."

The waiter eyed him suspiciously but decided to yield to his customer's request. He flipped it to Michael, who stared at both side of the coin intently. He knew a bit about rare coins; it was a hobby of his from childhood. He flipped it back to the waiter who caught it.

"Well, this is your lucky day," he said.

The waiter, suspicious, asked, "Why?"

"Unless I'm mistaken, it's an ancient Roman coin, and it's gold."

The waiter stared at him as if he was pulling a joke, decided he wasn't, and then quietly slipped the coin into his pocket.

Michael finished his meal in silence. Despite the lateness of the hour, he was in no hurry. Tomorrow would be Saturday; he could sleep late, and then put in a few hours at his office. He absentmindedly looked out the window and stared south down the dark street towards the loop. Very few people or cars were out and about. Out of the darkness of the night he saw a frail figure walking rapidly north towards the restaurant. He saw a woman dressed in dark blue, old blue scarf wrapped around her head and face. Michael thought, She looks like one of those Salvation Army workers I've seen.

As the woman progressed through the puddles of lights emanating from each light post, Michael was able to distinguish her features more clearly. It was Maria!

Michael jumped up from his booth and stepped through the revolving door, just as she was passing the entrance to the restaurant. She kept her head down and walked quickly. When she was about 15 feet away, Michael called out her name.

She stopped and slowly turned with a look of a frightened deer on her face. Their eyes locked. There was just enough light from the street lamps, and the restaurant itself, to clearly see each other.

"Maria," Michael stammered, "it's me, Michael."

A look of recognition flashed on her face but she stopped herself.

She and this man had never been properly introduced and her Latin heritage demanded that the proprieties be observed. Although she had never been with a man, to her it was unthinkable without the sacrament of marriage, she was still a woman, and she knew instinctively what all men were thinking; she decided to ignore him, to turn and resume her very rapid walk home.

As they stood frozen in time, staring at each other, neither Michael nor Maria realized that across the street, in the shadow of an alley, stood the white-haired man, observing them. The strange man made a small movement with his hand.

Over the coming years, Michael would often look back at this moment and have no idea why he did what he did. But in a voice that made his opponents in the courtroom wince, a voice that made the bureaucrats at City Hall jump, Michael commanded, "Maria! Come here!"

The young woman had never been spoken to that way, let alone by a stranger. She made up her mind to turn and run. But for a reason she would never understand, she stepped forward toward Michael and into…

the abyss.

CHAPTER THIRTEEN

She walked towards him as if she were walking on razor blades, her eyes never wandering from his. Michael's masculine intuition told him that if he made one false movement she would turn and flee. As a trial attorney he was well experienced in assessing and handling all types of people. He knew enough to step back when addressing an unknown female. It made her feel less threatened if he did so. He spoke to her with the lightest touch he could muster.

"Well, I thought it was you," he opened with a laugh in his voice. "What are you doing walking the street so late at night?" He watched her eyes carefully to make sure he had not inadvertently offended her. She stood four feet from him, but the posture of her body indicated she could bolt at any moment.

Finally, with hesitation, she responded, "I was just walking home."

"From the Loop?" he inquired, incredulously.

"Yes," she stammered.

"You must be frozen. I was just having a late night snack. He pointed through the glass window to his booth. Come on inside for a moment and have some coffee."

She started to decline his invitation but like a man used to people obeying him, he simply turned on as his heels and led the way back into the restaurant. She hesitatingly followed him.

When they were seated opposite each other in the corner booth, Michael continued his lighthearted chat while observing her intently. She was shaking, even indoors, away from the cold.

"I guess there aren't many buses running at this hour, you should have taken a taxi."

A look of confusion and embarrassment came over her face ever so briefly. "Oh, I prefer to walk," she said with a slight accent. "It's good exercise."

Years of experience questioning people on the witness stand told Michael she was telling a white lie, and it suddenly dawned on him. She probably didn't have the money for bus fare, much less a taxi.

"Well, you are absolutely right," he said, "it's good exercise in all types of weather. I was just finishing up a bowl of this excellent chili, I know you would enjoy some." Michael looked up at the waiter to indicate the new order. "And put on a piece of apple pie for me too." The waiter nodded and went to place the order.

Maria started. "No, no," she protested, "I don't need anything, I already ate."

Again, Michael perceived that she was fibbing. She was probably afraid of the bill. He looked at her carefully. She was underweight, frail. She was probably famished.

"Oh no, it's my treat," he said lightly. "You must try this chili! It really is very good." She shook her head no, but her eyes said yes. He ignored her denial and continued his innocuous conversation.

"Actually, I was walking home from a friend's house," he said. "I normally don't take this route since I live over by the lake. It's kind of ironic that we would bump into each other at this late hour."

Maria really didn't know what to answer. She was unfamiliar with situations like this. If Michael had been a client of hers – poor, displaced, sick, homeless - she would have known exactly what to say, how to say it, how to handle the situation. But this man was the opposite of all that. She glanced over him from time to time, noticing little details, like his gold watch. She had no idea what such a watch cost, but she knew it was expensive, and she knew she had never met a man who could afford one.

Michael noticed her glancing at it and with false humility explained it was a present from his law partners. He, of course, would never have thought of spending so much money on himself. Maria saw right through his false modesty, and she didn't like what she saw. She started to realize how out of her element she was. In her mind she began formulating an excuse to allow her to immediately leave the restaurant. But before she could execute her plan, their food arrived.

When Maria saw the size of the meal she began to protest again that she could never eat so much. Michael laughed and told her to give it her best shot. Slowly at first, then with increasing gusto, she dived into the meal. It flashed through Michael's mind that this might be the first meal that she had

had all day.

Michael ate his slice of apple pie as slowly as he could; he wanted this moment to last. Michael thought, this woman could not be more different me. He also realized that if his law partners saw him at this moment they would have been aghast that he was socializing at this hour with a member of the lowest socio-economic class of the city. But for once in his life he honestly didn't care. All he knew was that he was suffering from that great illness: loneliness.

While Maria ate, she never took her eyes off of him. She realized she was doing the same thing to him as he was to her. Both viewed each other as creatures from another planet. Every second, every moment, they were appraising, evaluating the other person.

It occurred to the young attorney, that despite this woman's innate beauty she probably had never been on a real date in her life. Little by little he coaxed her story out of her by what appeared to be innocuous questions. She revealed that she lived with her mother in a mostly Hispanic neighborhood that was not too far from Sarah's address. Her father had died young, but from time to time Maria talked as if he were still alive, as if the three of them were one happy family. She was born and raised in America, but her parents had emigrated here many years before. Contrary to Michael's expectations, she was not a full-time member of the Salvation Army. She was only one of the thousands of part-time workers that they hired for minimum wage during the holiday season. She liked the work raising money for the poor and working in the soup kitchen.

But Michael was fascinated to discover that her real job year round was as an L.P.N for a Catholic charitable institution. For some reason, Michael assumed it was probably a Catholic orphanage. So when Maria paused in her narrative, he asked, "I am sure it is your favorite part of the job, working with the children?"

She looked shocked. "Heavens no," she replied, "that's the hardest part."

"Why?" He asked, genuinely puzzled. "Where do you work?"

Her normally cheerful countenance was swept with a veil of sadness. "I work at St. John's Hospice," she quietly responded.

For once in his life, Michael was at a loss for words. He cast his eyes down at what was left of his meal, then out the window to the street and back again. Finally, when he had regained his composure, he glanced up and looked at Maria and with a shock he recognized the look on her face. It was one of sympathy for him! She realized that he had felt embarrassed by his question to her and her answer to him. But instead of feeling upset by the turn in the conversation she only felt sorry for making him feel ill at ease.

Their eyes locked on each other, both of them fully realize the gulf that existed between them. The differences of background, temperament, education, the very world in which each of them operated, it was as if they were solitary human beings alone in the world staring at each other over the vast expanse of the Grand Canyon. And yet, there was something....
...something between them.

For the briefest of seconds, Michael actually contemplated reaching out and holding her hand. Not out of lust, nor desire, but out of the need for understanding. Thankfully, he restrained himself from doing so. For as lonely as she was, she would never have tolerated such forwardness from a strange man.

They both realized it was time to go. Maria made her excuses that her mother was waiting for her and would be worried about her. Michael mentioned that he had to go to the office even though it was Saturday tomorrow. So he quickly paid the bill, giving the tired waiter a very large tip, and the two exited the restaurant together. As luck would have it a cab was slowly moving down the street looking for late-night fares. Michael waved him over. "Come on Maria, I'll give you a ride home." He opened the door for her. She began to protest vehemently. Michael took command of the situation.

"It is simply too late and too cold for you to continue to walk home. I have to go that way anyway," he lied. "Hop in." Maria still hesitated, but allowed herself to be manipulated into the cab, and in a few moments they were at her address, a dilapidated old apartment in an even worse neighborhood than Sarah's. Michael could tell by the dim light of the cab's interior that she was embarrassed by this location. He pretended not to notice, and wished her good night. He stated he was sure they would bump into each other again someday. As she quickly scrambled up the old concrete stairs of the apartment building, he memorized the address.

It had been a very long day with much to think about, but now he only wanted to go home and sleep. As he drifted off to sleep that night, Michael Barron had no idea of the complete turn his life had just taken.

CHAPTER FOURTEEN

The last few days of Michael's life finally caught up with him. He staggered in the front door of his condo, stripped off his clothes and plopped down into his bed. He was asleep the moment his head hit the pillow. He woke up at daylight and realized he had not turned once in his bed. He immediately fell back asleep and slept for several more hours.

When Michael finally awoke his body felt somewhat rested, but his mind was exhausted. He got up and made a larger than usual breakfast for himself. He carried his breakfast to the corner table where he could look out the expanse of windows that lined his condominium with a view that was almost 180 degrees. The snow had stopped, but it was one of those dark Chicago winter days in which one could not even guess at the hour. Due to the gray darkness the lake looked angry and forbidding with small whitecaps appearing further from the shore. But the great city with its new blanket of snow looked pristine.

He was having a hard time processing all that had occurred in the last few days. The hours of conversations with Sarah, the accidental meetings with the beautiful Latina girl Maria…it all gave him much to think about. He made a spur of the moment decision to visit a place he had not visited in quite some time, a north side cemetery, where several of his family members were buried. He dressed in casual clothes and left his home.

Being a lifelong resident of the metropolitan area, he knew the mass transit system like the back of his hand. With two connecting bus rides and a short walk he was at the gate to the old cemetery. It was noon, but in the gloom of the Chicago day it could have been mistaken for sunset. He passed through the old wrought-iron gate and walked down the gravel path to his family's tombstone. It was a large marble affair, ordered from Europe, with the name BARRON engraved in large letters on one side. His father had bought it for the family. A number of plots radiated out from the tombstone at the base of the large monument. On the base were engraved the names of his mother and father, side by side, with their dates. Next to them was his name with just his birth date and a dash.

In the past, the site of his tombstone had not affected him. But now, after the last few days, it appeared to him to have enormous significance. He thought of Sarah and her First Great Truth. But this day, this Christmas Eve day, staring down at his own mortality, for the first time he realized its true significance.

A movement some distance away caught his attention. He looked up and carefully surveyed the scene. He was not alone. Throughout this large old cemetery, the outlines of various human beings moved slowly. Men and women of all ages. All of them were alone. Some simply stood at a tombstone and stared. Some appeared to be praying. Others bent down and placed plastic flowers or evergreen wreaths on the object of their attention. But what struck Michael more than anything else was that each and every one was alone, on this day before Christmas.

He turned and began retracing his steps. The closer he got to the old iron gate, the faster he walked, for although he had been in the cemetery many times this was the first time he had experienced fear. Fear of what was yet to be.

❄ ❄ ❄ ❄ ❄

His mood did not improve until he entered the brightly lit and decorated lobby of his office building on Wacker Drive. When he stepped off the elevator and moved to the door of his office suite to open it, he discovered that the door had already been unlocked. He walked through the double doors into his office to find it brightly lit. Hard at work was his chief aide Joe Poleski. Joe looked up from his mountain of work, smiled brightly and said.

"Hello Mr. Barron. I didn't think you'd be coming in today."

Michael looked at Joe with new eyes. A few days ago he had decided to fire him after the Christmas break. As he entered his private corner office he couldn't help but reflect upon his own stupidity.

Where would I ever find another employee like Joe? He asked himself and then thought, This loyal sidekick is worth his weight in gold. It suddenly occurred to Michael that he had forgotten to do something. He had charged Joe with the onerous burden of buying Christmas gifts for everyone at his office, which of course, Joe had done with his normal efficiency and effectiveness. But here it was Christmas Eve, and Michael had forgotten about Joe. He sat down at his massive executive desk and a broad smile came upon his face. He unlocked the top drawer of his desk and took out his personal checkbook.

"Poleski! Get in here!" Michael barked. Joe limped into the office as fast as he could with a look of consternation and fear on his face.

"What is it, Mr. Barron?" He inquired, half pleading. "What mistake did I make?"

"The mistake you made, Mr. Poleski," replied Michael, "is that I gave you a direct order and you failed to carry it out!" The look on Poleski's face turned to one of terror. He had been waiting for this moment; he had heard the rumors that the firm was getting ready to discharge him. He knew he would never get another job as good as this one.

Michael continued as he leaned back in his chair and assumed his most threatening executive posture. "You know exactly what I'm talking about, Poleski!"

Joe froze in fear, unable to respond.

"I gave you a direct order to buy Christmas presents for everyone in this office, did I not?"

Joe's face turned to puzzlement. "But Mr. Barron, I did. I got everyone…"

"No you didn't!" screamed Michael, with mock anger. "You forgot the most important person in this office!"

Poleski looked as if he was going to faint.

"So as usual, I will have to do the most difficult job myself," stated Michael as he slammed his fist down on the desk. A broad smile slowly crept across Michael's face. "Merry Christmas, old buddy," he said quietly, and handed Joe the check.

Joe looked at the sum written on the check. He looked up at Michael and stammered in shock "Mister… Mister Barron… You must have made a mistake."

"Oh, you're right, Joe. I have made many mistakes concerning you. But starting Monday morning, we will rectify them."

CHAPTER FIFTEEN

He had to virtually pushed Joe out the office that afternoon. Joe insisted that there was much work to be done. But Michael insisted that it was Christmas Eve and that Joe should be home with his family. He of course knew his family was only his aged mother, though it was someone who loved him unconditionally. In his mind's eye he saw Joe rushing in the door of his modest apartment and announcing to the mother the size of his bonus check. For the first time in quite some time, Michael was genuinely happy.

"That is an order, Joe. Leave now! Monday morning, you and I will tackle this pile of work together. As always, we'll get it done on time." Joe's eyes were filling with tears of gratitude, and Michael, for all his macho mannerisms, was close to losing control himself.

"Tell your mother Merry Christmas from me," said Michael, and he turned quickly, walking back into his office. Joe saved them both the embarrassment by cleaning up his workspace and quickly exiting.

Michael stood in his corner office looking out the window. Well, for once I did the right thing, he thought with a halfhearted chuckle. He looked out over the darkening city in the late afternoon. Already the center of the city was deserted except for last-minute shoppers. He couldn't help but think of all the Christmas Eves he had enjoyed as a child. Back then, he had everything, not just wealth and comfort…but the love of a family.

Again, he thought of Joe. To Michael, Joe had always been a loser: poor health, no money, no future prospects. But this Christmas Eve, Michael was the loser. Joe had someone to go home to, someone who loved him unconditionally.

Michael immediately thought of Sarah. He had not made a conscious decision when he awoke this morning that he would spend Christmas Eve with this woman. But he knew he couldn't let her lie there alone as sick as she was without someone, him, to assuage the loneliness.

But for some reason he would never understand, his mind kept refocusing on Maria. He made an unconscious decision that on his way to Sarah's apartment that evening, he would walk by St. Peter's Church, and perhaps… well, he didn't know.

As he moved through the office turning off the lights and reflecting on the year just past, it suddenly occurred to him that he had nothing to bring Sarah on Christmas Eve. Maybe he could order some food in when he got to her apartment. As he was about to turn off the light in the little kitchenette in his office, Michael recalled Sarah's comments about Susan's oyster stew. He opened the refrigerator, and there was a large pot of the soup left over from the party before. He cleaned out a large coffee thermos and filled it with Susan's oyster stew. At least it was something Sarah might enjoy rather than letting it go to waste. Michael placed the large thermos into his briefcase, finished closing the office and departed for the long walk across the loop to his L station.

It was late afternoon and already dark. The loop was deserted except for suburbanites who had finished with their Christmas shopping and were walking to the train stations.

When Michael was two blocks away from St. Peter's Church, he began listening for the bell of the Salvation Army worker. But there was no sound, and as he drew closer to the front of the church the lights from within spilled out onto the sidewalk. He could clearly see the red iron stand from which the Salvation Army's red kettle normally hung. But the kettle was gone, and so was Maria. He was more disappointed than he thought he would be. He decided to push on towards his station. But something inside him told him to enter the church, and at the last moment he turned and climbed up the few short steps into the east door of the old church.

He nodded to the friar who was busy at a table in the lobby with the literature for the Christmas Eve service. Michael gingerly passed into the eastern aisle of the church and began walking down the long aisle towards the altar. He paused halfway down the church and stepped back slightly behind a large pillar. In the dim light of the partially lit church, he studied its occupants. All the usual occupants were there: the homeless who had no place to go and were forced to sleep sitting up in the pews, the old immigrant ladies mindlessly mumbling their rosaries, a few business people like himself perhaps on their way home from their offices.

But this day there were some unusual visitors: well-dressed, suburban families, small nuclear families, were wandering throughout the church. Michael surmised they'd finished their shopping and during their walk back to the train station had decided on a short visit to this old historic church probably more to show the young children the decorations than anything else. Or perhaps their visit was to show the younger generation where their immigrant ancestors had worshiped when they first came to Chicago from the old country.

Michael woke from these thoughts with a start. He had failed to notice that a choir had assembled at the front of the church and was launching into a musical rehearsal for the Christmas Eve masses. The Church began to fill with the beautiful music of old Christmas hymns. He decided to sit down in one of the empty pews and listen for a little while.

He sat down sideways in the pew with one arm over the back of the bench so that he could more closely observe the effects the music had on all the buildings occupants. But then out of the corner of his eye, in the gloom at the back of the church, he saw her.

Maria was dressed as always, in her dark blue uniform with a dark blue scarf around her head and her army style cap perched on the top of her head. She moved like an apparition slowly up the western aisle of the church carrying her little red kettle in front of her. Maybe it was the music, the setting, the fact that it was Christmas Eve, but he was thunder-struck by this sight.

Maria moved quietly, gently, up to the middle of the church where a niche in the western wall contained the nativity scene. Kneelers had been provided in front of the display. But the young woman chose to kneel at the side of it on the small steps that lead up to the Crèche.

Watching Maria's body language, Michael surmised she did not feel worthy to kneel directly in front of the Nativity. He watched her carefully as she assumed a kneeling position, her hands folded as if she were about to take her first Communion. He noticed with a start that she was positioned directly next to the statue of a life size angel. The statute looked down in adoration towards the empty cradle. Even in the dim light of the church he could monitor her expression as her loving gaze passed between the various plaster-of-Paris images, then settled with a look of yearning and sadness on the empty cradle.

When a young well-dressed suburban couple and their daughter approached the nativity scene and knelt on the well-padded kneeler in front of it, he observed Maria studying them carefully. In a flash of intuition, he understood the significance of it all to her. It was clear what Maria wanted for her life. And it was clear that up to this point in time, Fate had decreed otherwise.

Michael almost lost control of himself with this revelation. Every masculine instinct surged to the forefront of his being: the urge to protect, the urge to provide, the urge to comfort, to shield, to care for those whom he loved…all of this overwhelmed him, and he wanted to rush across the center of the church, to grab Maria and never let her go.

But a commotion at the front of the church broke his attention. A procession was forming, a procession of clergy led by a Monsignor in full regalia. In the procession, a young altar boy strained to carry the plaster image of the infant. The choir broke into the old hymn 'Adeste Fidelis' and the procession began its slow progress towards the nativity scene. Michael noticed that the people on that side of the church respectfully made way for this holy parade. He watched carefully Maria's reaction when she saw the procession of the high and mighty moving towards her. She instinctively grabbed the legs of a life-size statue of the angel as she slowly slid her body behind it as if to hide.

The procession stopped in front of the nativity scene, and after a raft of prayers the monsignor took the statue of the infant and placed him in the cradle. All gave a slight bow and the procession retraced its steps to the side door behind the altar. Slowly, the people in the church were drawn to the Crèche. The young suburban family resumed their position on the kneeler. Ever so cautiously, Maria slipped out from behind the statue of the angel and resumed her position of prayer.

Michael's gaze was fixated on Maria. He couldn't believe what he saw. At the side of this age old scene knelt the most beautiful image he had ever seen. Her body was erect; her hands were folded in perfect application with her head tilted slightly as she looked with an adoring glaze upon the infant. This was a scene worth painting by the world's great artists.

In the dim light of the church his eyes played tricks on him. He thought the angel had changed positions; it appeared that now the angel's adoring glance was on Maria. His outstretched hand appeared to have turned downward in blessing over the head of the young woman.

But something more was happening when he observed Maria's face. He noticed that it had changed. She no longer gazed at the figures in the manger rather her gaze had tilted upward towards the ceiling of the old church. With a start, Michael realized she was in some form of trance. A slight commotion caught his attention. It was the young daughter of the suburban couple kneeling at the front of the nativity scene. The daughter had become agitated. She was calling her mother's name, yanking at her sleeve and pointing at Maria. The mother at first ignored her and then seemed to chastise her daughter for causing a commotion. But the daughter would not stop. Finally, the mother turned to look towards Maria. She recoiled slightly in awe. She reached over to grab her husband's arm and tug on it. The young couple left the altar area immediately.

Michael found himself halfway across the church, walking slowly down the transverse aisle. He had lost all sense of self-consciousness. He moved like the proverbial moth to the flame. Soon he was a few feet from the kneeling figure of the Hispanic woman. She had remained frozen in her position, her eyes fixed without seeing on the ceiling of the church. Had the statue of the angel moved again? Michael glanced up at it. It appeared to threaten him as if to say, "This saintly woman is under my protection. Proceed no further, earthly man."

But no power on earth could have stopped this man from approaching this woman. He stepped forward and reached out his hands to cradle the head of Maria, stopping short of actually touching her.

As he leaned forward to look directly into her eyes, Maria appeared to suddenly come out of her trance. The look on her face told him she was shocked at seeing him there in the church so close to her. Inadvertently, she put out her hands against his chest to push him away. But then she stopped. Her right hand came to rest directly over his heart. Slowly, like a blind person probing the face of someone she did not know, she carefully and gently touched his chest. All creatures have their individual gifts, and hers was a gift of touch. Slowly, carefully, as she assessed his heart, the look on her face changed from fear to understanding.

But something inside Michael's chest changed, no, it broke. He had no idea why, but he knew his world had abruptly been altered . He suddenly recoiled backwards from Maria's touch as the tears began to burst from his eyes. He darted back across the church, grabbed his briefcase, and fled into the cold, dark Chicago night. The experience shook him to the core. This Latina, so different from him in every way, had completely destroyed his composure. As he ran down the steps of the church, he was little more than a frightened child; he was frightened of the unknown. And like a frightened child who had just been hurt, he ran for his home.

He ran for Sarah's apartment.

CHAPTER SIXTEEN

He paused momentarily outside the old, marred wooden door. The apartment building was deathly quiet. Normally the sounds of its occupants could be heard clearly in the hallway to Sarah's basement apartment. This evening, however, there was only the gurgling sound of the old steam plumbing. He gently knocked on the door. There was no response.

He tried the doorknob and as usual noticed it was unlocked. Slowly he pushed the door open inquiring as he did, "Sarah?" Only a small light remained on over the kitchen area. Sarah lay in the shadows in her normal position on the large double bed. For a moment Michael thought the worst had occurred, but then Sarah turned her head towards him and smiled weakly.

"How are you feeling tonight, Sarah?"

"Fine, just fine," she replied, but her strained breathing and weakened condition was alarmingly evident.

Michael turned on the light next to her bedside and sat down in the rocker. "Sarah, he began gently, I really must insist that we seek medical-" but Sarah cut him off abruptly.

"We have much to do this evening," she replied with determination.

Michael knew it was useless to fight this strong-willed old woman, so he decided to change his approach. "Well, it's Christmas Eve," he said in his most cheerful voice, "and things could always be worse!" He glanced sideways at her and saw the look on her face.

"Well, we'll have an outright party, then," he continued his effort at levity. "I brought you your first present of the night." He reached into his briefcase and brought out the large thermos of stew. "I present you with my secretary's ancient family recipe of oyster stew!"

He thought this present would elicit a groan of distaste from Sarah, but quite the opposite occurred. Her face lit up as if she were a little girl receiving a birthday present.

"Oh my," she said, "what a wonderful treat!"

Michael turned his face away so as to not reveal his surprise and amusement at her reaction. He decided to step over to the kitchen area and heat up the stew. As he did so Sarah pulled herself up in the bed and attempted to make herself presentable. It suddenly dawned on Michael, Sarah probably had not had anything other than the most basic foods for weeks and this truly to her would be a treat. He finished heating the stew and prepared a tray of two bowls and crackers and of course the mandatory tea. He brought the tray over, placed it with great flourish next to Sarah on the bed and assumed his normal position in the rocker.

Sarah dug into the stew with a gusto that absolutely surprised Michael. He feigned interest in the meal although he could barely choke it down. Finally Sarah paused and noticed with embarrassment that Michael had been watching her with amusement as she devoured her meal.

"I'm glad to see you're enjoying my present," Michael said.

Sarah paused and stared at him earnestly. After what seemed like an eternity of silence, she slowly began an explanation. "It's hard for any of us to understand what another person has been through," she stated reflectively. "You see Michael, when I was in the camp this Christmas stew of yours would have been considered a luxury surely worth dying for. Often for months on end all we had to eat was Bunkersuppen. You know what that is?"

He shook his head.

Sarah stared at the bookcase on the opposite wall as if peering through the decades into the past. A look of disgust spread across her face. "Bunker soup was made, Michael, by boiling a large pot of water and throwing into it any substance that could be digested by the human stomach. Leaves, grass, rotten vegetables that the guards didn't want, and any protein whatsoever." Sarah looked as if she was going to regurgitate.

Michael could picture the meat being carved off the rotten corpses of dead horses and rats.

"This soup, along with the thinnest slice of black bread was all we had to live on. This is why so many of the slave laborers did not survive, Michael." She could not go on.

Michael's face flushed red with embarrassment and shame. He was at a loss for words. They finished their meal in silence. When they were done, Michael spoke first. "Well then, there's only one thing to do," he said in his most cheerful manner. "Every Christmas Eve, you and I will meet and share a bowl of this fine oyster stew in memory of all those who have gone before us."

Her wise old eyes fixated on his. "I think that's an excellent idea, Michael, we must resolve to do just that." But they both knew the truth. In the future, Michael would be dining alone.

❄ ❄ ❄ ❄ ❄

The young lawyer quickly cleaned off the remains of their meal. As he did so, he glanced around the tiny apartment and realized for the first time that there was no television set, only an old radio sitting on the corner of one of the bookcases.

"How about some music around here?" He offered cheerfully. "After all it's Christmas Eve, and we should be more joyous." Then he checked himself. He realized that there would only be Christmas carols on most of the radio stations.

Sarah realized this fact simultaneously and said, "By all means. I love those old Christian hymns." Michael chuckled under his breath in amazement. What a remarkable woman, he flipped on the radio and spun the dial around until he found some soothing traditional Christmas music. Sarah nodded her head towards him in approval, and he resumed his seat in the rocker next to her bed.

Sarah glanced out the little window and noticed that the snow had begun to fall again. She turned to Michael and said, "What a cozy little scene we make in my old apartment." Michael heard the joking in her statement, but there was more truth than levity.

"Well, what should we talk about this evening he began?"

Sarah immediately responded, "Why don't you tell me what you did today?"

He was surprised by this statement, but then realized that Sarah was probably starved for contact with the outside world, so he resolved to provide it. He began an orderly exposition of the day's events: his half day at the office; the bonus check for old Joe; his visit to his family cemetery; his experience at St. Peter's Church. He stopped in his narrative, uncertain as to how to proceed.

Sarah was fully awake now. She was observing him in her peculiar way, hardly listening to his words but probing his mind and soul instead. She saw right through him, and his awkward silence. "I see we have now arrived at the most interesting part of your day."

Michael stammered out a response, trying to formulate his thoughts. "Well," he finally said, "there is this strange girl that I keep running into."

Sarah smiled. "Oh."

Michael proceeded to relate to her the occurrences of the last few days with the Salvation Army girl, Maria. Finally he arrived at the recent scene at the church. As he related what transpired inside the church he glanced at Sarah's face and was astounded by the laser light intensity with which she was following the story.

He finally concluded his story, paused, shrugged his shoulders and chuckled at the absurdity of it all. He expected a similar response from Sarah, but when he looked at her face, he saw that she was staring at him in deadly earnest. They lapsed into silence as they both broke their stare and gazed off in opposite directions.

When Michael glanced back at Sarah, he saw that she was staring with great intensity out the little window of her apartment as if she were trying to peer through the weak light far into the future.

Finally she turned to him. "I have just one question for you, my son."

Michael swallowed hard.

"Did you see her eyes? Did you look deep into her eyes?"

Michael started as if he had received a slight electrical shock. "I did…I did, and it was the most amazing thing."

"What did you feel, Michael?" She asked, softly.

He didn't know how to answer. He searched his mind for some time for the correct description of this strange experience. Finally he carefully replied, "When I looked into her eyes, Sarah, I felt, as if I had known her before. As if I had known her for a long, long time. What do you think it means?" He almost pleaded to the old lady.

Sarah leaned back in her bed and closed her eyes, as if she were debating exactly how much to tell him. Finally, she turned her face towards him and smiled. "It means, my dear young friend, that you may have received the most important Christmas present…

....Of your life."

PART THE FIFTH

CHAPTER SEVENTEEN

Men have but a short time to live
Homer

Michael noticed with alarm the change in Sarah's color and the difficulty with which she was breathing. His visit thus far seemed to exhaust her. "Do you have any coffee?"

She motioned to the cupboard in the little kitchen area.

He said, "I think I'll make some coffee while you rest."

He glanced back from his task in the kitchen to notice that she appeared to be sound asleep already. Good, he thought, I'll let her rest. He filled his mug with the fresh brew and return to the rocker, which he repositioned so that he could face the small basement window. The Christmas music played softly from the old radio as he gazed out at the light snow falling on the sidewalk in front of Sarah's building. He sat there gently rocking, drinking his coffee and holding Sarah's hand while she slept.

Christmas Eve, he thought. What would my friends and associates think if they could see me now? But, then again, he fully realized that this was the one night of the year when loneliness is most keenly felt and the warmth of human companionship most highly valued.

His mind drifted back over the events of the last few days. How strange it all was, especially his meeting with this old woman and how quickly she had become an integral part of his life.

He began mentally to review the hours of conversation he had had with Sarah. He glanced around the room at the hundreds of volumes it held and it began to dawn on him exactly how much work, how much time, it must have taken Sarah to absorb and to digest all of the great ideas contained in her library. He realized for the first time what a first-class intellect he was dealing with.

Slowly, as he began to review their conversations he understood that no matter how far a field they might have gone, Sarah always gently guided him back to her central theme, the Four Great Truths.

So far they had discussed two of them. Both had seen so mundane as to hardly be worthy of discussion, but upon reflection he understood the immense ramifications each implied.

But something was wrong with all of this, intellectually wrong. Up until this moment it had nagged on him, but he couldn't put it into words. Now it was evident to him the truths were fine as far as they went. But the underlying contradiction was not addressed. Sarah's view implied an all knowing, all loving, all-powerful God, Creator, Spiritus Mundi. But how could any such ultimate being allow its creatures to suffer, to grope through the darkness of the centuries, to experience unspeakable evils? Look what Sarah had been through. How could any loving Spiritus Mundi allow that to happen?

There it is, Michael thought, there it is! There is no way for Sarah to explain this "Great Truth" of life on this planet!

Sarah awoke. "Oh my, it looks like I dozed off again for a moment."

"That's quite all right," said Michael, "it's good for you."

"Would you like a cup of coffee?"

Sarah nodded, and Michael got her coffee and then resumed his normal position.

"While you were napping, Sarah, I reviewed our discussions of the last few nights concerning your Great Truths. And, I think I found a serious flaw in your argument!" Michael still liked the idea of being able to outwit the wise old woman.

Sarah's eyebrows rose while she smiled at Michael. "Oh?" She finally said. "I am always up for a challenge."

Michael gathered his thoughts for a moment and then began "You see Sarah, the heart of your philosophy is that there was, or is, a Creator. A divine being, a Spiritus Mundi that created this universe, and His invisible hand somehow guides it all along. The problem with that is that such a divine being would not allow His creatures to suffer. He would not tolerate evil. He certainly could not stand idly by and watch the terrible horrors of this century that you have observed firsthand."

Sarah waited for Michael to continue.

"I mean," the young lawyer stammered, "this divine being would have to be all good, all-knowing, all loving. Right?" He checked himself with his own thoughts. "Unless, of course, you want to assume an opposing Being, an evil god, a devil, which is the root cause of all of our evil-" Michael trailed off, lost in his own thoughts. After a few moments, he thought aloud, "I wonder if anybody has seriously considered that possibility?"

Sarah couldn't help herself, and she broke out into a repressed laugh. "Well actually, it has occurred to a few others that the solution you suggest to this problem of evil in the world is best presented with the assumption of an equally powerful evil being."

"Oh," was all Michael could say.

"As a matter of fact," Sarah continued, trying to control herself, "the Zoroastrians posited such a duality, good and evil Gods, thousands of years ago. And of course, more recently, our Judeo-Christian philosophers have maintained the existence of an extremely powerful evil spirit and his legions. Which I believe you refer to as Satan."

Though the young lawyer and the old scholar both loved a good intellectual argument, and they were just warming to the cause, Sarah abruptly waved off further debate with a quick movement of her hand.

"This subject, Michael, has been debated in professional philosophical circles for millennia."

Michael of course realized she was right. He paused for a moment and looked carefully at the old woman's face. His skills as an attorney told him intuitively that she was exercising about one tenth of her intellect, playing with his mind like that of a grammar school teacher.

He decided to step back and assume a different position. "It's clear to me," he said, "you have studied long and hard on all of these subjects, and you have the advantage over me in this territory."

Sarah looked away, modestly.

"Perhaps then, you can tell me how you explain this difficulty I have raised, this dilemma we all face in acknowledging the incredible amount of evil in this world."

"If I could do that young man, I would win the Nobel Prize!" Sarah joked.

"Well, you must believe in some solution to this problem," the young attorney responded.

Sarah simply gazed out the small window and did not answer.

This was such a key matter that Michael could not let it rest. "I read some time ago," he began, "that there were several different attempts made to assassinate Adolf Hitler. How easy it would have been for your Creator to intervene in history at such moments. Could He not have acted or sent an agent to act in his place to assure the elimination of such evil? If any of these plots had succeeded, perhaps the Holocaust could have been completely avoided."

"So," Michael said, warming to the attack, "here is a clear case of God causing evil or at least allowing it to happen."

Sarah simply stared at him.

"Or," Michael continued, attempting to be objective, "perhaps it is the case that God simply allowed the evil side of the universe, the devil, to work his will amongst us poor human beings."

Sarah continued to intensely stare at him.

"I mean," Michael continued, "it's one or the other. Either a divine being causes or allows such evil, or a very powerful evil being causes such evil to exist in this world. You have to agree with that, Sarah!"

She simply responded, "No."

"Well, there has to be a cause of it!" He blurted. "Things don't happen completely randomly, you would be the first to admit!"

"I agree with your last statement," she said somberly.

"Well then," the prominent attorney stated with a certainty he normally reserved for a successful summation in a courtroom, "Who would you maintain is responsible for these great evils like the Holocaust?"

Sarah pinned him with her eyes, and after a few intense moments, finally responded,

"You… and Me."

CHAPTER EIGHTEEN

Even though it was almost midnight, Sarah was wide-awake. Her color had improved somewhat but her breathing was still labored. Michael debated whether he should head for home, but then thought he would wait until Sarah was sound asleep for the night. Clearly Sarah enjoyed having the young lawyer by her side, especially on this night of all nights.

"You mentioned," the old lady began, "that you have been thinking about our first two truths. I am somewhat surprised that you are not more curious about the remainder of the Four Great Truths."

"Oh, I am," he responded. "I just didn't want to push you."

"Well then," she replied cheerfully, "we must forge ahead. Now that you have had sufficient time to absorb the first two truths and their implications you should be filled with a need, an emptiness, when you consider your own life in relationship to what you have learned."

Michael became lost in thought. "Yes," he finally responded, "I suppose you're right."

"Precisely so," said Sarah. "The first two Great Truths may allow you to assess your place in this universe, to understand the direction we are all going and fully appreciate that no matter how bleak this world may seem we all have been given the greatest gift of all, the greatest succor: hope!"

"But the real question, now that you understand all this, is why are you, as an individual, allowed to live one more day when so many tonight will pass on? In short, what is the meaning of your existence in this world? What is your destiny? What are you to accomplish in the remaining hours, days, or years of your earthly existence?"

Michael simply stared at the old woman. He was in awe of her insightful mind. In a flash he understood that she had stated the human dilemma with precision. "I am sure you are going to tell me," he responded, with a slight degree of sarcasm. He hated feeling so unintelligent.

Sarah chuckled. "Well, you must admit it is certainly a topic worthy of discussion."

He nodded his agreement. "Actually, it's a topic I have given some thought to," Michael stated. "It's always seemed to me that there are two types of people in this world. The first type, from a very early age, plan both their short and long-term futures. They are always working towards their goals. Indeed, they take the time to formulate their goals.

"The second type of person, well, his/her life just seems to be one long series of accidents. Their jobs, the people they choose to marry, their short-range accomplishments, appear to occur almost at random."

Sarah nodded at his observation and smiled slightly. "Yes," she said, "it almost appears as if some of us have a destiny, whereas others of us are simply victims of chance."

"Exactly!" Michael exclaimed. "Exactly!"

Sarah was clearly enjoying this conversation, so he decided to play it out to its logical conclusion.

"I guess if you really think about this," he continued, "it all boils down to whether we each have a destiny or not. And if so, who determines this destiny for each of us?"

Sarah looked exceedingly pleased that her young visitor was finally thinking clearly. "It is a topic that has been debated for centuries," the old gentlewoman started, "And one's answer to this puzzle will determine many things, indeed everything!"

"I see," Michael responded, but of course he did not.

"Over the centuries, great thinkers have discussed this problem in many different ways. Free will versus determinism, the meaning of life, how one is to find meaning within one's life. It's all different approaches to the same issue.

"The real difference between the two types of people you have noticed Michael, is that the first group has a clear idea, or at least they think they have, of their place in this world and their ultimate destiny."

"Obviously," the attorney responded, "but living life on a day-to-day basis is hard enough with everyone facing a multitude of choices every day. What seems like an insignificant decision may lead them down a path to their personal fulfillment." Michael smiled. "Or their destruction."

"Granted," Sarah responded. "And it is equally obvious that if one has clear ideas on this subject for their own life, their struggle to fulfill their goals will be greatly simplified."

"Granted," Michael responded, with a slight degree of mockery. His attempt at levity was lost on Sarah, who sat quietly by. "Okay, okay," he finally said, in all seriousness, "I think I get what you're trying to say."

"Good," the old woman cagily responded. "Why don't you summarize our discussions so far?"

Michael rose to the bait. "Let's see. Your first truth teaches us about the shared human condition we all face on this earth. No matter who we are, what our background is, what distinctions we may hold, we are all traveling down the same road of life together, and we will wind up at the same destination, a destination that acknowledges no distinctions between human beings. The implications of this truth are many and far-reaching, but the overwhelming import of this is the view of equality and tolerance we should have for each other. The negative implication of this, however, is the obvious fact that, 'Vanity, vanity, all is vanity.' In other words, what good does it do a man or woman to struggle to accomplish, to accumulate, to persevere through all the obstacles of life, when the only thing we will own, the only thing we will be able to claim at the end of our all too brief life is our graves.

"Obviously these sorts of reflections on our history as a species, our treatment of our fellow human beings, our shared future can only lead to one thing: despair. So, the second truth is that we cast around looking for any ray of hope, any explanation, anything that might lift us from this despair. And in the dark of the night the universe answers us, with the cry of a newborn baby. Instinctively we know that the universe, or nature, or 'God,' if you will, has not given up on us.

"And at this time of year both believers and nonbelievers are forced to reflect on one such baby born 2000 years ago. Thus, the Second Great Truth teaches us that there will always be one candle still burning in the darkest of winter nights. A candle that gives us the light of hope."

Michael had been staring, as if in a daze, at the wall above Sarah's head as he recited his summary of the First Two Great Truths. He glanced back at Sarah's face and was inwardly pleased at the look of approval and satisfaction with which she smiled at him.

"Well done, young man," she said. "I see that our time together has not been wasted."

Michael looked away, blushing slightly from the praise.

"So, now we come to the Third Great Truth," the gentlewoman said with a flourish. "The basis of this truth is, as with the first two truths, both simple and obvious. As you have correctly surmised the question we now face, once we accept the first two truths; what are we to do with the rest of our lives? How are we to find meaning? How are we to find our destiny if indeed we have one?

"You are absolutely right when you say there are two types of people. Of course this is an oversimplification, but the fact of the matter is some people's lives appear to occur as mere reactions to forces around them, a series of accidents as you put it. And then, there are other people who seem to constantly work, struggle, and often achieve their goals as if they had something or someone guiding them, a road map to follow. Am I stating your position correctly?"

Michael nodded.

"Good," she responded. "We may actually cover quite some distance this evening. Or should I say before sunrise?" Sarah had glanced at her clock and noticed it was already past midnight. "I think the Third Great Truth will allow you to begin, Michael, to see the world clearly. Then you will finally be ready for the ultimate secret to your life, the Fourth Great Truth."

Michael realized this was the first time Sarah had mentioned the Fourth Truth. He decided to gently press her on this. "Is this fourth truth more important than any of the others?"

Sarah gently said, "Yes."

Michael decided silence was his best tactic. He diverted his gaze to the wall and remained in his most reflective professional position.

Sarah saw through the ruse. "All in good time," she said. "All in good time. As a matter of fact, the Fourth Great Truth is best learned through experience. It is not something that I can simply..."

Michael continued to stare at the wall in order to encourage Sarah to keep talking. After a few seconds he heard a loud gasp from his dear friend. He glanced back at her face and was shocked to see a look of surprise and horror. She was staring intently at the little window that looked out upon the street.

"What's wrong? Sarah, what's wrong?" He almost screamed as he rotated his body around to stare at the window. He just caught a glimpse of a figure withdrawing from view.

If he could have seen what Sarah saw, he would have been equally shocked. She had seen the face of a man pressed up against the window staring intently at her. He had white hair, alabaster skin, and what appeared to be tinted glasses. The look on his face was one of utmost earnestness. In the short time that Sarah had watched his face she could see he was mouthing one word over and over to her. When she finally understood the word, she panicked.

For the white-haired man was imploring her…

"Hurry! Hurry!"

CHAPTER NINETEEN

"**G**et control of yourself, Sarah! Get control of yourself!" Michael screamed. The old lady was thrashing and churning violently in her bed. Michael had to grab her by the shoulders and force her back down. "It's okay," he kept repeating. "It's okay, nothing will harm you."

But in truth, he was just as alarmed as she was. He had no idea what she had seen at the window that would so upset her, but Sarah saw the situation clearly. "There is no time left, Michael! There is no time left!" And she began to thrash again.

"Sarah!" He commanded. "You have to calm down, or else I'm calling an ambulance."

Sarah looked at his face and knew that he meant it. She used her last bit of willpower to gain control of herself. "A glass of water, Michael, a glass of water, if you would. And maybe some tea, also."

Michael jumped at the task. He was glad to have something, anything, to do to calm his friend. What in the world did she see in that window? He thought. It was probably just some old derelict looking for a warm place to stay for the night, he assured himself.

Sarah drank the cold glass of water in one long draw and began sipping a large mug of hot tea that Michael had procured for her. She became agitated again as she stared between the little window and Michael's face. With the utmost effort she regained her composure.

"We have much work to do," she said at last, "much to discuss. You have yet to learn the Third and Fourth Great Truths before the sun comes up today."

It occurred to Michael briefly that she might finally be losing her mind. Sarah paused for the longest time, staring with intensity at the bookcases opposite her bed. Michael could tell she was ordering her thoughts like an computer, sifting and winnowing through mounds of data.

She began. "There is no more time for our little Socratic game of questions and answers." The intensity of her eyes shook Michael . The mask she had been wearing these many long hours of conversation, the mask that made her appear to be simply an old lady of limited intelligence and knowledge, fell to the ground like a pane of glass shattering.

Michael saw in an instant the rare intelligence, the genius, the wisdom gained from years of study and experience; it was more than enough intellectual power to equal any other human being he had ever met.

"You have correctly stated the essence of the first two truths, although you have missed some of the implications," Sarah continued, "and you have clearly perceived that the problem we are left with is what the philosophers through the ages have referred to as 'the meaning of life.'

"There is not a person who has ever crawled across the face of this earth that hasn't wondered why he or she was born. We have all labored away trying to make our way in this world invariably wondering what possible meaning there could be to all this and indeed, why should we go on at all?"

"To be or not to be," Michael quoted the Bard contemplatively.

"Right," she responded. "And as you have also correctly stated, some people seem to find an answer to all of this for themselves, they seem to find their own destiny and work towards it while the rest of humanity stumbles from one accidental occurrence to the next." Sarah paused for a long drink of her tea. Michael sat quietly like her obedient pupil, and at this moment in time, he was. With a few careful glances Michael could clearly see that Sarah was trying to be as concise as possible.

She began again on what seemed to be a wholly new track. "Michael," she said, "one of the most important things you can understand about yourself and your fellow travelers is that we are all comprised of three basic elements. The first is, of course, the physical. Our physical well-being will determine much of our happiness and success in this world. Secondly, there is the psychological. The importance of psychological health is so obvious we need not even pause at this point in our discussions to consider it. The third element is equally important with the first two, but is more and more ignored in the modernity of our time. I am referring to the spiritual component of every human being.

"Now, how an individual formulates and cares for the spiritual side of his nature is something each of us has to discover for ourselves, just as one picks the best exercise routine or the best educational program for the other components of our nature. But this you must never doubt: all three components of a human being are of equal value and must be kept in balance for one to achieve his or her full potential; to live life to its fullest as his or her creator meant. In short, to define and fulfill one's destiny."

For a long time there was silence between these very different human beings as they each stared off in different directions, both deep in contemplation.

"You see Michael," she began again, "we human beings are like these new guided missiles. In order for them to work correctly, all the parts must be in perfect balance, and they must lock onto the signals, the communications, which their creators and controllers are sending to them constantly. We used to use an expression: 'on the beam,' and this is what was meant.

"Human beings are very similar to this. We need to lock onto the signals from our Creator. We need to get on the beam in order to discover and work towards our destiny.

"Thus you can see how, to some people, it appears that we invent our own meaning in this life, but to other people it appears our destiny is laid out for us. Both views are partially correct."

"I think I see," the young attorney responded. "But how is one supposed to get the signals? How is one supposed to get on the beam, so to speak?"

"It varies for each person, Michael. The traditional answer would be prayer or meditation or contemplation, but above all acknowledging that we as individuals are irrevocably linked to the Spiritus Mundi. Without His guidance we are lost."

"And with it?" Michael asked.

"We have a better chance of understanding and achieving our destiny. No guarantees, of course, but a better chance at it. In the end, it's still all up to us."

"Is this part of the Third Great Truth?" He asked.

"It *is* the Third Great Truth," she responded. "This truth states that all three components of a human being: the physical, the psychological and the spiritual must be acknowledged and nurtured. The purpose and function of the spiritual part of the human being is to connect us to the will of the Creator. We can of course ignore this; we can of course refuse to make the connection. But only in doing so will all of our talents and powers be brought to fruition, to achieve the purpose for which we were created.

This is why, my son, none of us should ever be afraid of death, only of a life wasted.

❋ ❋ ❋ ❋ ❋

Sarah was so exhausted by her exertions she fell asleep sitting up. Michael glanced at the clock by her bedside and then turned to gaze out the small basement window. It was the middle of the night, only a few hours before sunrise. The streets of the city were almost completely deserted. No one was out, except for those who had to be: policeman, firemen, city workers.

On this coldest and darkest night of the long year, an eerie quiet blanketed the great city. Even the bars closed early this night and people had no place to go but their homes. Children lay in their bed blissfully unaware of the agony many others were going through this night: the lonely, the desperate, the abandoned, and above all, the suicidal. This night of all nights, human beings needed each other, and loneliness was the greatest burden. Michael sensed all of this as he held Sarah's hand and listened to the wind sweeping through the canyons of the dark city.

He thought for a moment that perhaps he should go to his condo despite the lateness of the hour. But then he looked at Sarah, his dear, dear Sarah. She should not be alone this night, nor should he. Besides, he had much to think about.

Michael's mind drifted back over the last few days. So much had happened it seemed as if an eternity had past since he first discovered Sarah in that dark alley. Their conversations over the last few days had shaken him to the roots; no, they had torn out his roots, upending his previous belief system about himself, the world, and his fellow human beings, and instilling a completely new one.

He knew that not enough time had passed for him to thoroughly digest what he had learned, what had happened to him. Perhaps what was most alarming was that over the last few days it seemed as if he lost control over his life, and that something or someone was directing his very steps. That strange girl that he had met was a perfect example: Maria... Maria...

He must have dozed off in the old rocker during his reflections for he was abruptly awakened by the erratic movements and sounds of Sarah in her bed. It was only a short time before sunrise, and he was genuinely glad that this long night was over. Until he looked at Sarah.

She had awoken in an agitated state, her breathing was extremely difficult, her color a deathly white. Michael decided that enough was enough.

"We are going to the hospital now, Sarah! Whether you want to or not!" She smiled weakly, as she glanced quickly out the small basement window.

"No," she whispered, "it is too late."

"But Sarah..." Michael tried to continue.

"Listen to me," she said, "we have not yet discussed the Fourth Great Truth, it is the capstone of all the truths. It is the one truth, the only truth, which will bring you peace in this sorry old world. I can tell you what it is but it is a truth best learned through experience." At this point, she was barely able to whisper. And a few moments later, even whispering was too much exertion for her.

She pointed to her Bible, and Michael picked it up off the side table and handed it to her. Then she pointed to her old overcoat hanging on a hook behind the door and motioned for her young pupil to bring it to her.

He gently laid it across her. She pointed to the sprig of evergreen on the wooden chip that was pinned to her lapel. She motioned to Michael's lapel. He transferred the memento to his own chest.

Sarah once again motioned between the Evergreen sprig and her Bible. Michael thought he understood. "Do these contain the Fourth Great Truth?" He asked her gently as he stroked her brow. She nodded her head and Michael beamed at the slight smile on her face. She was very proud of her student.

The grand old woman struggled to speak but could not. Her time had come, as it comes to all creatures. She knew it and so did Michael. Her labored breathing became less and less frequent as she prepared for her journey.

With a howl, like a wounded animal, Michael broke into tears and laid his head upon his friend's chest. Had he been able to see all of reality, he would have seen the form of a beautiful young Jewish girl rise gently from the bed and stand behind him, looking down upon him with the utmost benevolence, and love. Instead, as he wept in the arms of the forever still Sarah, he felt a slight draft run through his hair.

Of course, he did not see the hand of the young Jewish girl stroke his head in benediction and farewell, before she turned and gently disappeared into...

the shadows.

CHAPTER TWENTY

The CPD paddy wagon rumbled slowly down the predawn street. Sgt. Cronin sat in the passenger seat and let his young partner do the driving. Cronin was two years from retirement and 60 pounds overweight. He had pulled this "meat wagon" detail on the Christmas graveyard shift because he had dared to question his new watch commander. The only thing that kept him going day after day nowadays was the thought of finishing up his career. Two years, he thought.

"There it is," the young officer said, spotting the numbers on Sarah's apartment building. With a squeal of the old brakes, the wagon double-parked directly in front of the door. Cronin and his partner hauled out the collapsible gurney and opened the ancient door into the lobby.

"It's a basement apartment," the partner said, glancing at his clipboard. They negotiated the gurney down the few short steps into the hallway. Michael had left the door open to Sarah's apartment, and he stepped out into the hallway immediately upon hearing the clatter. "This way, officers."

Cronin carried the gurney into the small apartment and set it up next to the bed. He flipped open the metal cover of his clipboard and began gathering the information from Michael while his partner checked the body under the sheet to confirm its condition.

"Name?" Cronin asked, barely looking from the clipboard as Michael told him his friend's name. Cronin had done this so many times he knew the form by heart. On this detail, there were only so many variables and after all these years of hauling out the dead, there was no emotion, no feeling, in the old officer. It was just a job, and he was checking off the days, like a kid waiting for Christmas. His wife joked that his retirement was the only thing that made him smile any more.

Michael supplied all the information he could, and then he handed the sergeant his business card. "I will be responsible for all expenses, for arranging all the details, just give me a call."

The sergeant snorted. Yeah sure, I'll call you on Christmas day, Cronin thought. He informed Michael that the remains would be at the county morgue on the west side of the city. Michael would have to call and make the necessary arrangements himself.

Michael Barron could not watch the proceedings, so he turned away and pretended to look out the window while the two officers quickly wrapped and deposited the body on the gurney. Without a word, they labored away to remove the old woman up the stairs, out the door, and into the back of their wagon. As they were getting into the squadrol, the old cop stopped and turned to look at Michael, who had followed them out the door. It was clear to the cop that this young man was not directly related to the deceased, but he cast a look at Michael and asked, "Family?"

Without hesitation, the young attorney simply responded, "Yes."

As the paddy wagon slowly disappeared down the dark street, Michael turned and reentered Sarah's apartment. There, lying on the corner of her bed was her Bible. He picked it up and bent it just enough to fit into the large side pocket of his overcoat. This book and the souvenir from Auschwitz he had pinned on his lapel were the only thing he took with him. He turned off the lights and closed the door for the last time.

❄ ❄ ❄ ❄ ❄

Michael Barron stepped out into the cold predawn air. For a moment, he stood on the sidewalk lost in thought. He turned east towards the lake and began walking slowly. Picking up speed it occurred to him that he would have to walk all the way to his condominium, the streets were still virtually deserted. When he arrived at the main north-south Avenue he should have turned right towards his home. Instead he staggered like a drunken man across the intersection and continued east to Lake Michigan.

His head so full of thoughts, of recollections over the last few days, he barely realized what he was doing. Sarah's Great Truths swam endlessly in his mind as he tried to make sense of it all. And this Fourth Great Truth! She had said it was the capstone of it all. She maintained it was more important than the other three truths combined, that it was the only thing that would bring ultimate happiness to a human being. The wise old woman had told him he would have to learn it from experience. She had left him only two clues, both of which he carried with him; the sprig of Evergreen stapled to the wooden chip pinned on his lapel and her Bible.

And what about that strange girl that he had met, this Maria? Why couldn't he get her out of his mind? Why did Sarah see the importance of their meeting, but he could not? He would probably never see her again, so what difference could it possibly make? But those eyes of hers, as long as he lived he would never forget those eyes.

As he passed the numerous alleyways he was startled to see three homeless men huddled around a makeshift fire burning in an old oil drum. Michael stopped, frozen by the realization of the unjust gap between his life and theirs. Silently he stepped into the alley and up to the huddled men. He removed his prized watch and gave it to the startled assembly. "Merry Christmas," was all he said. He realized that in the future he would have no need of such things.

He continued to stagger down the street through the slush on the sidewalk towards a small strip of sandy beach at the lake. Two buildings away from the end of the Avenue, Michael passed a darkened alleyway where mercifully, for his own sanity, he did not see the white-haired man step from the alley as he walked past. The albino watched him intensely as he walked towards the lake. A smile crept across the man's face, and then he turned and disappeared into the darkness at the back of the alley.

Michael reached the little beach and stepped out onto the frozen sand. As he did so the first rays of the sun, the glorious sun, broke over the lake and began to illuminate the darkened canyons of the great city.

Barron stepped slowly across the beach to the very edge of the icy water. The lake was completely calm, reflecting light like a mirrored tabletop. Michael, the lake, the city itself were soon brilliantly lit by the half-risen sun as it appeared to climb out of the water on the far shore of the lake.

Dawn burned into his eyes. The sun blinded him, and with its feeble warmth, the young man understood for the first time the importance of what had transpired during the last few days. Although a losing battle, the sun still pushed back at the cold winter air. And although it might be a losing battle for him also, he knew that no matter how difficult, he had no choice but to incorporate and practice the first Three Great Truths in his life from this day forth. And he knew he would spend the rest of his life searching for the secret of the Fourth Great Truth. How all of this would transpire, he had no idea. But on that cold Christmas morning he fell to his knees, into the shallow water at the edge of the lake. He spread his arms in acceptance and bowed his head in submission. There was only one thing that he knew for certain. His life had changed…

Forever.